Boston Public Library, American Assoc. of University Women

Contributions Towards a Bibliography of the Higher

Education of Women

.

Boston Public Library, American Assoc. of University Women

Contributions Towards a Bibliography of the Higher Education of Women

ISBN/EAN: 9783337158637

Printed in Europe, USA, Canada, Australia, Japan

Cover: Foto ©Paul-Georg Meister /pixelio.de

More available books at **www.hansebooks.com**

CONTRIBUTIONS

TOWARDS

A BIBLIOGRAPHY

OF THE

HIGHER EDUCATION OF WOMEN.

Compiled by a Committee

of the

Association of Collegiate Alumnæ.

———— ·•◆•· ————

BOSTON:
The Trustees of the Public Library.
1897.

PREFACE.

Mr. Herbert Putnam,

   Librarian of the Boston Public Library:

   Dear Sir—

   While expressing on behalf of the Association of Collegiate Alumnæ its hearty appreciation of the courtesy extended by the Trustees of the Boston Public Library in consenting to assume the responsibility of publishing the Bibliography of the Higher Education of Women, I beg the privilege of making mention here of the thanks due to those individual members of the Association who have contributed freely of their time and labor towards gathering, recording and classifying the references relating to the education of women. These the Association now passes over to your care, with the belief that the skilled and experienced oversight that will be given to their publication will add to its value.

   The increasing number of requests coming to the officers of the Association for information as to the history, development and value of the higher education for women made it evident that there existed a need for a full and accurate compilation of all available literature on the subject.

   Believing that the library facilities in and around Boston offered the best chance for securing such information as was desired, the Association recommended that the Boston branch should undertake the work of preparing a Bibliography. The initial step towards bringing together the catalogue was taken by a committee of the Branch under the direction of Miss Eliza P. Huntington who was obliged later, on account of sickness, to resign her place, and the charge then fell to Miss Mary H. Rollins. At the suggestion of Mrs. Martha Foote Crow, director of the Bureau of Collegiate Information, Miss Rollins agreed to carry on the work as a sub-committee of the Bureau, and in that capacity was able to secure an appropriation for clerical assistance from the General Association to complete the work.

   It is to the patient and untiring industry of Miss Rollins that the present compilation is largely due.

   On behalf of the Association of Collegiate Alumnæ,

Very respectfully,

Annie Howes Barus,

Secretary.

February, 1897.

EDITOR'S PREFACE

The phrase "higher education" is admittedly unhappy, but its use in the present connection is not indefensible. Such a list as the following, to be of value, cannot ignore the historical side of its subject. It must, therefore, take account of much early material, which, viewed in the light of present conditions, seems to have little bearing on the phase of the question under consideration; and, for this reason, it is fortunate that we have a term the significance of which has varied from decade to decade. In other words, the relativity of the phrase used in the title is its justification here.

It was the original intention of the committee to include among the American colleges in Section VII. only those which belong to the Association of Collegiate Alumnæ; but it was felt that the interesting and important part played by certain other institutions in the development of the movement justified the committee in including them. The dates which follow the names of these colleges show the year in which they were opened to women.

Most of the accompanying titles are such as the members of the committee have been able to verify in the libraries at hand. A few others, however, which seemed of special interest, have been inserted, although the committee cannot vouch for their accuracy. The numbers attached to many of these titles are the shelf-numbers of the Boston Public Library, and the initials P R indicate that the bound volumes of the magazine cited are kept in the Periodical Room of this Library. The list has been arranged according to the following scheme:

I.   General and Historical.
II.   Higher Education in Relation to Health.
       This includes physical education and the question of the mental inferiority of women.
III.   Coeducation.
IV.   Professional and Scientific Education.
       Law.
       Medicine.
       The Ministry.
       Science.
V.   Post-Graduate Study.
VI.   Occupations and Opportunities for College-Bred Women.
VII.   Colleges and Universities wholly or partly Open to Women.
VIII. Societies for the Education or Advancement of Women.
       Author Index.

The editor welcomes any corrections or suggestions.

Mary Harris Rollins.

Boston Public Library,

May 1, 1897.

A BIBLIOGRAPHY

OF THE

HIGHER EDUCATION OF WOMEN.

I. General and Historical.

A. The influence and education of women. Colburn's New monthly magazine, 34: 227. 1832.   P R

Abbott, Lyman. The education of women. (The woman's book, pp. 337–355. 1894.)
4003.121

Abbott, Wilbur C. Higher education of women in England. Nation, 63: 26. 1896.
P R

Adams, Mrs. Charles Kendall. The highest education. (World's congress of representative women, pp. 131–134. 1894.)   5583.14

Adams, Herbert Baxter. History in colleges for women. Vassar, Wellesley, Smith, Bryn Mawr. (In his Study of history in American colleges, pp. 210–228. 1887.)   7593.55
Published as Circular of information, no. 2, 1887, of the U. S. Bureau of education [*7596.59 (1887)].

Adams, William Henry Davenport. Woman's work and worth in girlhood, maidenhood, and wifehood. With * * * chapters on the higher education and employment of women. London, 1880.   3576.77

Adhémar, Vicomtesse d'. Nouvelle éducation de la femme dans les classes cultivées. Paris, 1896.   3599.47

Advancement of women. Chautauquan, 11: 474. 1890.   P R

Advancing influence of women. Spectator, 58: 1132. 1885.   P R
Remarks on a paper by Llewelyn Davies.

Aitken, Edith. College life for women. Sunday magazine, 25: 99. 1896.   P R

Alcott, Amos Bronson. Woman. A conversation. Radical, 5: 89. 1869.   *7302.2.5

Alden, Leonard Case. Woman in college. Harvard magazine, 6: 353. 1860.
A humorous poem in reply may be found in the same magazine, Oct., 1860 [*4398.5.7].

Aldis, Mary Steadman. Complements and compliments. Westminster review, 136: 173. 1891.   P R
— Thou art the man. Contemporary review, 63: 387. 1893.   P R
Concerning degrees for women.
— Women's education in New Zealand. (Proceedings of the International congress of education, Chicago, 1893, pp. 883–886.)
*3592.145

Alfonso, Nicolo d'. The problem of woman's education. Trans. by Victoria Champlin. Education, 6: 361, 420. 1886.   P R

Allen, William Francis, and David E. Spencer. Higher education in Wisconsin. Washington, 1889. Illus. [U. S. Bureau of education. Circular of information, 1889, no. 1.]
4496.324
With bibliographical lists.

Almy, Emma A. A year's progress for college women. Education, 10: 476. 1890.   P R

American college manual. A handbook of information concerning the principal American institutions of learning for the higher education of young men and women. Compiled and edited by C. Powell Karr. N. Y., 1889.

Anderson, Rufus. An address [on the education of the female sex] delivered at the second anniversary of Mount Holyoke seminary. Boston, 1830.   4498.150

Arjuzon, C. d'. L'éducation des femmes il y a cent ans. Paris, 1893.

Arndt, Ernst Moritz. Briefe an Psychidion, oder: Ueber weibliche Erziehung. Altona, 1819.   No. 8 in 7594.56

Backus, Helen Hiscock. Some recent phases in the development of American colleges. Abstract of a paper presented to the Association of collegiate alumnæ. [Brooklyn, 1889.]

Bacon, G. A. [Review of the correspondence in the Nation relative to entrance examinations in women's colleges.] The [Syracuse] Academy, 3: 252. 1888.   P R

Banks, Elizabeth L. Self-help among American college girls. Nineteenth century, 39: 502. 1896.   P R

Barbauld, Anna Lætitia. On female studies. (Works, vol. 2, pp. 235–243. 1826.)   4577.66.2
See also other editions of her Works.

Barnard, Frederick Augustus Porter. The higher education of women. Passages extracted from the annual reports of the president of Columbia college, 1879, 1880, and 1881. N. Y., 1882.

Barrau, Caroline de. La femme et l'éducation. Paris, 1870.   3579.52

Bates, Octavia W. Women in colleges. (Papers read before the Association for the advancement of women, 1892, pp. 15–21.)
7572.70
Beale, Dorothea. A few words of retrospect and forecast. (Proceedings of the International congress of education, Chicago, 1893, pp. 862–864.)   *3592.145
— Girls' schools past and present. Nineteenth century, 23: 541. 1888.   P R
— The Ladies' college at Cheltenham. (Transactions of the National association for the promotion of social science, 1866, pp. 274–287.)   *5566.3 (1866)
— On the education of girls. By a Utopian. Fraser's magazine, 74: 509. 1866.   P R
— Organization of higher education for girls. (International conference on education. Proceedings, 1884, pp. 327–362.) 3763.100.16
With discussion.
— University examinations for girls. (Transactions of the National association for the promotion of social science, 1875, pp. 478–490.)   *5566.3 (1875)
Beedy, Mary E. Girls and women in England and America. (Brackett, Anna C. The education of American girls, pp. 211–254. 1874.)   3599.161
— Higher education of women in England. College Courant, 12: 39. 1873.   *7290.3.12
Belloc, Bessie Rayner Parkes. Remarks on the education of girls. London, 1854.
— Same. 2d ed. 1856.
Benneson, Cora Agnes. The college education of women. Journal of pedagogy, 8: 13. 1894.
Partially reprinted under the title Health of college women, in the New England kitchen magazine, 3: 66. 1895.
Better education for women. Monthly religious magazine, 47: 183. 1872. *5397.1.47
Bisson, Frederick Shirley Dumaresq de Carteret. Our schools and colleges. London, 1872.   5599.52
— Same. Vol. 2. For girls. [London.] [1884.]   5599.84.2
Blackburn, Helen. How may the higher education of women be most efficiently advanced in Ireland? (Transactions of the National association for the promotion of social science, 1882, pp. 422–425.)
*5566.3 (1882)
— ed. A handbook for women engaged in social and political work. New ed. Bristol, 1895.   5588.129
Pt. 3, pp. 49–69, devoted to the education and employment of women.
Blaikie, W. G. Woman's battle in Great Britain. North American review, 163: 282. 1896.   P R
Blake, Sophia Jex. A visit to some American schools and colleges. London, 1867. 3598.65
Describes Oberlin, Hillsdale, and Antioch; with an added chapter on coeducation.
Blanc, Thérèse. The condition of women in the United States. Trans. by Abby L. Alger. Boston, 1895.   5588.105
Pp. 165–224 deal with colleges for women, coeducation, etc.
Blathwayt, Raymond. The education of our girls. A talk with Miss Buss. Cassell's family magazine, 1: 306. 1894. *7352.1.1

Boardman, George Nye. Female education: the importance of public institutions for the education of young women. An address before the officers and students of Mount Holyoke seminary. N. Y., 1867.
No. 30 in *5590a.61
Reprinted from Hours at home, 5: 491, 1867 [P R], where it was published under the title "The importance of public institutions for the education of young women."
Bölte, Amely. Female education and culture in Germany. Massachusetts teacher, 24: 343. 1871.   *5286.1.24
Bolton, Sarah Knowles. Social studies in England. Boston. [1886.]   3577.36
Contains chapters on the Higher education of women at Cambridge, at Oxford, in London University, and in University College, Women in the art schools, etc.
Boone, Richard G. Education in the United States. N. Y., 1889. [International education series.]   3599.101
— Same. 1894.   3599.152
The higher education of women, pp. 362–382.
Boyer, L. University women. Nation, 59: 212. 1894.   P R
Bracchi, S. Educazione della donna. Piacenza, 1890.
Brackett, Anna Callender, editor. The education of American girls. N. Y., 1874.
3599.161
Contents: Brackett, A. C.: Education of American girls. Cheney, E. D.: A mother's thought. Dall, C. H.: The other side. Stone, L. H.: Effects of mental growth. Beedy, M. E.: Girls and women in England and America. Jacobi, M. P.: Mental action and physical health. Hamlin, S. D.: Michigan university. Nutting, M. O.: Mount Holyoke seminary. Johnston, A. A. F.: Oberlin college. Avery, A. C.: Vassar college. Antioch college. Rood, O. N.: Letter from a German woman. Brackett, A. C.: Review of "Sex in education." Appendix.
— Woman and the higher education. N. Y., 1893.   3589.119
Essays by Mrs. E. Willard, Mrs. E. C. Embury, Maria Mitchell, Mrs. L. G. Runkle, Mrs. A. F. Palmer, Lucy M. Salmon, and Anna C. Brackett.
Bremner, C. S. Education of girls and women in Great Britain. With a preface by Miss E. P. Hughes. London, 1897.
Bristol, Augusta C. Philosophy of women's era. Victoria magazine, 28: 378. 1877. P R
Broadhurst, Thomas. Female education. Edinburgh review, 15: 299. 1810.   P R
Reprinted in Selections from the Edinburgh review, 3: 374. 1835 [4573.138.3].
Browne, George Forrest. An imperial university for women. Nineteenth century, 33: 857. 1893.   P R
Bryce, James. Progress of female education in England. Nation, 37: 10. 1883.   P R
Bryce, Marian. A plea for the higher education of women. Catholic presbyterian, 4: 401. 1880.
Buckle, Henry Thomas. The influence of women on the progress of knowledge. (Essays, pp. 165–209. 1863.)   4558.5
Buisson, Benjamin. De l'enseignement supérieur des femmes en Angleterre, en Écosse et en Irlande. Revue internationale de l'enseignement, 5: 30, 238, 488. 1883.
Bullock, Alexander Hamilton. The centennial situation of woman. Address. Worcester, 1876.   4485.146
Burns, Alexander. Female education in Ontario. (U. S. Bureau of education. Special report. Educational exhibits and conven-

tions at the exposition, New Orleans, 1884–85, pp. 437–441.)   *7590a.72

Burroughs, Charles. An address on female education, delivered in Portsmouth, N. H. Portsmouth. [1827.]   No. 8 in 7590a.14
Reviewed in the Western monthly review, 1: 626. 1828 [*5296.1.1].

Burstall, Sara Annie. The education of girls in the United States. London, 1894.
   3598.143

Burton, John. Lectures on female education and manners. 2d ed. London, 1793. 2 v. Vol. 1 is on 5599a.84.

— Same. 5th American ed. Elizabethtown, 1799.   5599a.17

Bury, J. B. Women at the doors of the universities. Saturday review, 81: 269. 1896. P R

Butler, Josephine E., editor. Woman's work and woman's culture. Essays. London, 1869.   5573.34
Reviewed in the Nation, 9: 342 [P R].

Byers, Mrs. How may the higher education of women be most efficiently advanced in Ireland? (Transactions of the National association for the promotion of social science, 1882, pp. 413–422.)   *5566.3 (1882)

Campo-Grande, Viscount de. Woman, her moral and political influence. Education, 4: 633. 1884.   P R

Capes, John Moore. Women. Victoria magazine, 18: 261. 1872.   P R

Caplin, Roxey A., and Mill, John. The higher education of women. (Women in the reign of Queen Victoria, pp. 403–444. 1876.)
   3578.85

Carey, Francis King. Women of the twentieth century. Princeton review, 1884 (2): 105, 324.   P R

Certificates to the university. Nation, 64: 8. 1897.   P R

Chapman, Mary Francis. A plea for women. [By J. C. Ayrton, pseud.] Victoria magazine, 14: 97. 1869.   P R

Charruand, D. The education of women in France. Unitarian review, 22: 151, 225. 1884.   P R

Claghorn, Kate Holladay. College training for women. Outlook, 55: 546–844. 1897. P R
The article is divided into five parts as follows:
1. What may be expected from it, p. 546. 2. The preparation, p. 599. 3. Choosing a college, p. 751. 4. Life at college, p. 792. 5. The transition to the world, p. 844.

Clark, Sylvia. The higher education of woman in America. New England magazine, 8: 711. 1890.   P R

Clough, Anne Jemima. English university life for women. Forum, 12: 358. 1891. P R

Cobbe, Frances Power. The defects of women and how to remedy them. Putnam's monthly magazine, 14: 226. 1869.   *5285.1.14

— Female education and how it would be affected by university examinations. London, 1862.   No. 4 in *7579.38

— Same. (Essays on the pursuits of women, pp. 216–239. 1863.)   3574.18

Cohn, Gustav. Die deutsche Frauenbewegung. Deutsche Rundschau, 86: 404; 87: 47, 264. 1896.   P R

College doors opening. Every Saturday, 11: 363. 1871.   P R

College entrance examinations. Journal of education, 45: 49. 1897.   *7590.8.45

College woman, The, and the home. Leslie's illustrated weekly, 83: 343. 1896. *6941.15.83

College year-book and athletic record for the academic year 1896–97. Compiled and edited by Edwin Emerson, jr. N.Y., 1897. 4490a.124

Collegiate training for women. Critic, 14: 364. 1890.   P R

Commission of colleges in New England on admission examinations. Annual report, 1st–10th. 1886/87–95/96. Providence, 1887–96.   *7592.75

Commonplace papers about women. St. James's magazine, 28: 528, 604.

Cone, Kate Morris. The gifts of women to educational institutions. A paper read before the Association of collegiate alumnæ, Oct. 25, 1884.

Constantia, pseud. Defense of American women. Portfolio, 20: 276. 1818. *3200.20.20
A defense of their intellectual standard.

Conway, Moncure Daniel. The education of girls in England. Radical, 7: 301. 1870.
   *7302.2.7

Cooke, George Willis. The intellectual development of women. Unitarian, 3: 387. 1888.   *7503.50.3

Crawford, Emily. The education and status of women [in France, England, and America]. Subjects of the day, 1: 116. 1890.

Cronyn, David. Woman as a mendicant. Radical, 3: 382. 1868.   *7302.2.3

Crow, Martha Foote. Facilities for the university education of women in England. (U. S. Bureau of education. Report of the commissioner for 1894/95, vol. 1, pp. 805–891.)   *7595.1 (1894/95), vol. 1

— Women in European universities. Nation, 54: 247. 1892.   P R

Curtis, George William. Address [on the development of the higher education of women]. (Addresses at the celebration of the 25th academic year of Vassar college, pp. 22–64. 1890.)   4490.209

Cushman, Robert Woodward. American female education: what? and by whom? Boston, 1855.   5599a 91

Cymon, pseud. Thoughts on the proposed improvement of female education. Christian observer, 7: 295, 361. 1808.   P R

Dall, Caroline Wells Healey. The college, the market, and the court; or, woman's relation to education, labor, and law. Boston, 1867.   5576.18
Reviewed by Elizabeth Cady Stanton in the Radical, 3: 343. 1868 [7302.2.3].

— Historical pictures retouched. Boston, 1860.   4506.75
The women of Bologna, pp. 85–134; The contributions of women to medical science, pp. 135–168; Marie Cunitz, the mathematician, pp. 198–206.

Dana, Henrietta Channing. What French girls study. Atlantic monthly, 69: 204. 1892.   P R

Darwin, Erasmus. A plan for the conduct of female education in boarding schools. Derby, 1797.

— Same. Added, Rudiments of taste. Phila., 1798.

Davies, Emily. The application of funds to the education of girls. A paper read before the education department of the National association for the promotion of social science. London, 1865.   5566.6

— The higher education of women. London, 1866. 5599a.40
Reviewed in the Nation, 3: 426 [P R].
— Special systems of education for women. Victoria magazine, 11: 356. 1868. P R
— Women in the universities of England and Scotland. Cambridge, 1896. 3597.159
Davies, John Llewellyn. The advance of women. Read at a church conference, 3d July, 1884. (Social questions, pp. 327–353. 1886.) 3586.90
Davis, Emerson. [Female education.] An address delivered at the sixteenth anniversary of the Mt. Holyoke female seminary. Northampton, 1853. 4498.151
Davis, Horace. Collegiate education of women. Overland monthly, 16: 337. 1890. P R
Davis, Paulina Wright. On the education of females. Read at the convention at Worcester, Mass., Oct. 16, 1851. [Syracuse, N. Y., 1853. Woman's rights tracts, no. 3.] *5573.31
Dawson, Sir John William. Thoughts on the higher education of women. Nature, 4: 515. 1871. P R
Extract from the Introductory lecture to the Ladies' educational association of Montreal.
Day, Henry Noble. An address on education: at the annual commencement of [the Ohio female college]. College Hill, 1859. 4496.201
De Foe, Daniel. An academy for women. (An essay upon projects, pp. 282–304. 1697.) **3648.2
Dike, Samuel Warren. Sociology in the higher education of women. [Boston, 1892.] 3572.121
Reprinted from the Atlantic monthly, 70: 668. 1892 [P R].
Dix, Morgan. Lectures on the calling of a Christian woman, and her training to fulfil it. N. Y., 1883. 3589.79
Lecture iii: The education of woman for her work. Reviewed in the Popular science monthly, 23: 120, 409 [P R].
Drayton, Eunice. New wine in old bottles. Lippincott's monthly magazine, 3: 161. 1869. P R
Dühring, Eugen Karl. Der Weg zur höheren Berufsbildung der Frauen und die Lehrweise der Universitäten. Leipzig, 1877. 3570a.72
Dugard, Marie. La société américaine. Paris, 1896. 4368.153
Dupanloup, Félix Antoine Philibert. La femme studieuse. Paris, 1870. 5579a.97
— Same. 4e éd. 1880. 5574.96
— Lettres sur l'éducation des filles et sur les études qui conviennent aux femmes dans le monde. Paris, 1879. 3594.54
— Studious women. London, 1868. 5585.84
— Same. Trans. by R. M. Phillimore. Boston, 1869. 5585.83
Reviewed in the Christian remembrancer, 55: 416. 1868 [P R]
Eastman, Mary F. The education of women in the Eastern states. (Meyer, Annie N., ed. Woman's work in America, pp. 3–53. 1891.) 3575.119
Edselas, F. M. How to solve a great problem [the higher education of Catholic girls]. Catholic world, 56: 353. 1892. P R
Education and influence of woman. Southern review, 8: 406. 1870. P R

Education of girls. Victoria magazine, 33: 168. 1879. P R
Remarks on "Schools for girls and colleges for women," by C. E. Pascoe.
Education of girls; their admissibility to universities. Westminster review, 109: 56. 1878. P R
Reprinted in Littell's living age, 136: 685 [P R].
Education of woman. American review, 4: 416. 1846. *5215.1.4
Education of women. Dublin university magazine, 3: 583. 1874. P R
Education of women. Edinburgh review, 166: 89. 1887. P R
Education of women. Nation, 3: 165. 1866. P R
Review of Essays on the pursuits of women, by Frances Power Cobbe.
Education of women. Nature, 10: 395. 1874. P R
Education of women in England. Unitarian review, 7: 431. 1877. P R
Edwards, Bela Bates. An address at the fourth anniversary of the Mount Holyoke female seminary. Andover, 1841. 4495.261
On the history of the education of women.
Eggleston, George Cary. The education of women. Harper's New monthly magazine. 67: 292. 1883. P R
Eliot, Charles William. Collegiate education for women. Extracts from [his] address at Smith college. New England journal of education, 9: 409. 1879. P R
— Elective studies for women. An address delivered at the first commencement of Smith college at Northampton. Springfield daily republican, June 19, 1879.
Eliot, William Greenleaf. Education of girls and young women. A lecture delivered at Washington university, St. Louis. [1876.] 7592.100
Elmond, pseud. Hints respecting the education of females. Christian observer, 7: 432. 1808. P R
Embury, Emma Catherine. An address on female education, read at the anniversary of the Brooklyn collegiate institute for young ladies. N. Y., 1831. No. 10 in *7592.67
Emerson, George Barrell. A lecture on the education of females, delivered before the American institute of instruction. Boston, 1831.
Reprinted from the Lectures before the Institute [3593.1(1831)].
Englishwoman at school. Quarterly review, 146: 40. 1878. P R
Reprinted in Littell's living age, 138: 451 [P R].
Entrance requirements in women's colleges. [Correspondence.] Nation, 46: 269, 298, 320. 1888. P R
Eubule-Evans, A. Position of women in Germany. Victoria magazine, 22: 193. 1874. P R
Fabeck, L. Van Sittart de. The making of woman. Westminster review, 145: 544. 1896. P R
Faithfull, Emily. Three visits to America. Edinburgh, 1884. 4367.66
— [Women and work. With discussion.] Victoria magazine, 23: 191. 1874. P R
Fawcett, Millicent Garrett. The education of women of the middle and upper classes. Macmillan's magazine, 17: 511. 1868. P R
Reprinted in the Eclectic magazine, 71: 828 [P R].

— The future of English women. A reply. Nineteenth century, 4: 347. 1878. P R
— University education for women in England. (Proceedings of the International congress of education, Chicago, 1893, pp. 853–862.) *3592.145
— The use of higher education to women. Address to the students of Bedford college. Contemporary review, 50: 719. 1886. P R
Reprinted in Littell's living age, 171: 729. 1886 [P R]; also in the Critic, 10: 272. 1887 [P R].
Felmeri, Louis. Higher education for girls in Hungary. New England journal of education, 5: 268. 1877. *7590.8.5
Female education. (Kiddle, Henry, and Alexander J. Schem, editors. Cyclopædia of education, pp. 299–304. 1877.) 3592.55
— Same. (In same. 3d ed. 1883.) 3592.64
Female education. Christian observer, 69: 655. 1869. P R
Female education. Quarterly review, 119:499. 1866. P R
Female education. Quarterly review, 126: 448. 1869. P R
Female education. Circular of the Ladies' collegiate institute. Amherst, 1854. 4499a.48
Female education, good, bad, and indifferent. National quarterly review, 4: 267. 1862. P R
Female education in Massachusetts. American journal of education, 30: 581. 1880. P R
Female poaching on male preserves. Westminster review, 129: 290. 1888. P R
Female suffrage and education. Nation, 5: 152. 1867. P R
Feminine knowledge. Victoria magazine, 9: 99. 1867. P R
Fénelon. De l'éducation des filles. Texte revu sur l'édition originale (1687) et publié avec une introduction et des notes par A. Gasté. Paris, 1882.
— Instructions for the education of a daughter done into English and revised by George Hickes. 4th ed. London, 1721. 5599a.34
— Treatise on the education of daughters. Trans. and adapted to English readers. By T. F. Dibdin. Albany, 1806. 5599.72
— Same. Boston, 1821. 3599.34
— Same. 1831. 3574.38
Festivals in American colleges for women. Century, 49: 429. 1895. P R
Fitch, J. G. The education of women. Victoria magazine, 2: 432. 1864. P R
— Women and the universities. Contemporary review, 48: 240. 1890. P R
Flack, Alonzo. Diplomas for women. (Proceedings of the second anniversary of the University convocation of the state of New York, 1865, pp. 155–158.) *6361.2.2
Frank, Louis. University opportunities for women. Educational review, 8: 471. 1894. P R
Franklin, Christine Ladd. The education of women in the Southern states. (Meyer, Annie N., ed. Woman's work in America, pp. 89–106. 1891.) 3575.119
— The higher education for women. Century, 53: 315. 1896. P R
On the attitude of Mr. Romanes.
French, Frances Graham. Educational status of women in different countries. (U. S. Bureau of education. Report of the commissioner for 1894/95, vol. 1, pp. 893–976.) *7595.1 (1894/95), vol. 1
G., S. Effects of female improvement on domestic happiness. Christian observer, 7: 155. 1808. P R
Gallaudet, Thomas Hopkins. An address on female education, Nov. 21, 1827, at the opening of the new edifice of the Hartford female seminary. Hartford, 1828.
Gardner, Alice. A transition period in female education. Modern review, 5: 70. 1884. P R
Garnett, James Mercer. Lectures on female education. 1st and 2d series. 3d ed. Richmond, 1825. *7589.1
Gilman, Arthur. Collegiate instruction for women. Journal of social science, 24: 68. 1888. P R
— Women who go to college. Century, 36: 714. 1888. P R
Girls in the public schools of Boston. American journal of education, 13: 243. 1863. P R
Goddard, Matilda, compiler. [Articles and items concerning women and their work. 1890–95. Scrapbooks.] 23 v. **5581.1
These volumes, although possessing no bibliographical interest or existence even, are full of valuable material.
Gould, Elizabeth Porter. The woman problem. Education, 12: 73. 1891. P R
Grant, Sir Alexander, bart. Happiness and utility as promoted by the higher education of women: an address delivered [before] the Edinburgh ladies' educational association. Edinburgh, 1872.
— Reform of women's education in Great Britain. Princeton review, n. s., 5: 344. 1880. P R
Grant, George Monro. Education and co-education. Canadian monthly, 16: 509. 1879. P R
Gray, Alonzo. An address on female education, read at the annual commencement of the Brooklyn Heights seminary. N. Y., 1854. No. 5 in *5574.29
Great lawsuit, The. Man v. men, woman v. women. Dial, 4: 1. 1843. *5235.4.4
Grey, Maria Georgina. The woman's educational movement [in England]. (Stanton, T., editor. The woman question in Europe, pp. 30–62. 1884.) 3572.53
— and Emily Shirreff. Thoughts on self-culture, addressed to women. Boston, 1851. 5599.62
Reviewed by Charles Card Smith in the Christian examiner, 51: 185.
Gulick, Alice Gordon. A woman's college in Spain. (Transactions of the National council of women, 1891, pp. 189–192.) *5583.13
Gurney, Mary. Are we to have education for our middle-class girls? Or, the history of Camden collegiate schools. 3d ed. London, 1872. [National union for improving the education of women of all classes. No. 2.] No. 2 in *7599.82
Hall, Lucy Mabel. Higher education of women and the family. Popular science monthly, 30: 612. 1887. P R
An answer, in part, to the address of Dr. Withers Moore, British medical journal, 1886 (2): 295.
Ham, Charles H. The education of women a prime necessity. (Manual training, pp. 123–129. 1886.) 5597.68

Hamilton, William T. A plea for the liberal education of woman: an address at the annual exhibition of the Female seminary, at Marion, Ala. N. Y., 1845. No. 15 in *7592.67

Hanscom, Elizabeth During. The administration of collegiate beneficiary funds and scholarships. A paper read before the Association of collegiate alumnæ. [Washington? 1892.]

Harkness, John C. The normal principles of education. An address delivered in part before the American normal association, and suppressed by the acting president and assistant presiding officer on the ground that it is too strong an advocacy of "woman's rights." 3d ed. Trenton, 1863.
No. 20 in *5595.66

Harris, Samuel. The complete academic education of females. New Englander, 11: 295. 1853.   P R

Harrison, Mrs. Frederic. An educational interlude. Fortnightly review, 65: 359. 1896.   P R

Hayes, Alice. Entrance requirements in women's colleges. Nation, 46: 256. 1888.   P R
Opposes admission by certificates. See replies on pp. 279, 298 and 320 of the same volume.

Herford, W. H. Female education in the middle class. Theological review, 3: 526. 1866.

Higginson, Thomas Wentworth. The American girl-graduate. Critic, 9: 273. 1886. P R
— The fear of its being wasted [i.e., the higher education]. (Women and men, pp. 232–237. 1888.)   4409a.145
See also the chapter on "Chances."
— The ghost of a chance. Harper's bazar, 29: 482. 1896.   *5400.1.29
— Higher education of woman. A paper read before the Social science convention. Boston, 1873. [Woman suffrage tracts, no. 9.]
— Same. Journal of social science, 5: 36. 1873.   P R
— Ought women to learn the alphabet? Atlantic monthly, 3: 137. 1859.   P R
— Same. (Atlantic essays, pp. 93–121. 1871.)   6017.79
— Woman and her wishes; an essay. Boston, 1853.   No. 7 in *3443.24
— Same. 2d ed. With appendix. N. Y., 1853.   No. 8 in *3443.24
— Same. [3d Amer. ed. Boston, 1854? Women's rights tracts. No. 4.] No. 4 in *3579.129
— Same. (Series of women's rights tracts. Rochester.)   No. 12 in *5576.3

[Higher courses for women at the university of St. Petersburgh.] Nation, 64: 33. 1897.   P R

Higher education for women. Journal of education, 24: 421. 1886.   7590.8.24

Higher education for women in Germany. Nation, 49: 426, 446. 1889.   P R

Higher education of women. Eclectic magazine, 110: 536. 1888.   P R

Higher education of women. English woman's domestic magazine, 15: 135. 1873. P R

Higher education of women. Nation, 3: 426. 1866.   P R
A review of "The higher education of women," by Emily Davies.

Higher education of women. Penn monthly, 8: 255. 1877.   P R

Higher education of women. (U. S. Bureau of education. Report of the commissioner for 1889/90, vol. 2, pp. 743–754.)
     *7595.1 (1889/90), vol. 2

Higher education of women. Westminster review, 129: 152. 1888.   P R

Higher education of women. 1. What has been done for it in Scotland. 2. The question of its advantages. Chambers's journal, 5th series, 4: 33, 134. 1887.   P R

Higher education of women in England. Letters from Emily Sharpe and Mary E. Beedy. Unitarian review, 1: 379. 1879.   P R

Hippeau, Célestin. L'éducation des femmes et des affranchis en Amérique. Revue des deux mondes, 2e pér., 83: 450. 1869.   P R

Hodgson, William Ballantyne. The education of girls (considered in connection with the university local examinations). Victoria magazine, 3: 250. 1864.   P R

Hopkins, John Henry. On female education. (American citizen, pp. 354–376. 1857.)
     4429.18

Hoskins, James Thornton. Female education. Victoria magazine, 16: 299. 1871.   P R
— Women's rights. Victoria magazine, 18: 349. 1872.   P R

Howe, Elizabeth Mehaffey. Women's colleges and college women. Christian union, 39: 239. 1889.   P R

Influence of university degrees on the education of women. Victoria magazine, 1: 260. 1863.   P R

Ireland and female progress. Victoria magazine, 26: 237. 1876.   P R

Jacobi, Mary Putnam. Higher education of women. Science, 18: 295. 1894.   P R
Calling attention to the opening of Barnard college, and opposing a secluded, gregarious college life for girls.

James, Henry. Woman, and the woman's movement. Putnam's monthly magazine, 1: 279. 1853.   P R

Janet, Paul Alexandre René. L'éducation des femmes. Revue des deux mondes, 59 (3. pér.): 48. 1883.   P R

Jenner, G. Women at the Swiss universities. Fortnightly review, 24: 339. 1868.   P R

Johnston, William. An address on female education. Columbus, 1845.

Jones, Charles Edgeworth. Education in Georgia. Washington, 1889. Illus. [U. S. Bureau of education. Circular of information, 1888, no. 4.]   3592.118
Contains a sketch of the Georgia (now Wesleyan) female college, the first college in the world to confer a degree upon a woman, pp. 90–101; also, shorter notices of some twenty other educational institutions for women.

Kelley, Florence. Admission of women to universities. International review, 14: 130. 1883.   P R
This article grew out of an unsuccessful application for admission to the University of Pennsylvania, and contains strictures upon a letter written from the University point of view by Mr. Francis A Jackson, dean of the faculty of arts; with a reprint of the letter.
— Exiled from our native land. [Letter on the opportunities for women at Zürich.] Woman's journal, Aug. 22, 1885.   *7260.51
— Zürich for American women students. Woman's journal, Aug. 1, 1885.   *7260.51

Kettler, J. Das erste deutsche Mädchengymnasium. Weimar, 1893. [Bibliothek der Frauenfrage.]
— Was wird aus unsern Töchtern? Weimar, 1889.
— The woman question in Germany: translated from Was wird aus unsern Töchtern? Chautauquan, 10: 708. 1890. P R
King, Alice. Thoughts on female education. Argosy, 9: 431. 1870. P R
Kingscote, Georgiana. A Brahmin schoolgirl. Nineteenth century, 25: 133. 1889. P R
Knatchbull-Hugessen, Eva. The higher education of women. National review, 13: 33. 1889. P R
Král, J. J. Comenius on the education of women. Nation, 54: 412. 1892. P R
L., M. A. E. The girl of the future. Victoria magazine, 15: 440, 491. 1870. P R
Lage, Bertha von der. Das höhere Mädchenschulwesen Frankreichs seit der Republik. Berlin, 1885. [Deutsche Zeit- und Streit-Fragen.] No. 12 in *5216.50.14
Lander, E. T. University examinations for women. Education, 1: 48. 1880. P R
Lange, Helene. Frauenbildung. Berlin, 1889.
— Higher education of women in Europe. N. Y., 1890. [International education series.] 3597.103
Contains a list of higher educational institutions open to women. Reviewed by Helen Hiscock Backus in the Educational review, 1: 84. 1891 [P R].
— Rede zur Eröffnung der Realkurse für Frauen. Berlin, 1889. 7596.87
Laveleye, Émile Louis Victor de. L'instruction supérieure pour les femmes. Revue de belgique, 42: 272. 1882. P R
Lazarus, Josephine. Higher education: a word to women. Century, 41: 315. 1890–91. P R
Le Conte, Joseph. An address delivered on commencement day of the Laurensville female college. Laurensville, S. C., 1860. 4497.101
The running title is "Female education."
Lee, A. L. The "impasse" of women. Westminster review, 141: 566. 1894. P R
Lewis, ——. Woman's position, past, present, and future. Victoria magazine, 17: 227. 1870. P R
Lewis, Amelia. A real education for women. Dark Blue, 2: 620, 756; 3: 288. 1872. *7317.50.2, 3
Liberal education for women. Harper's New monthly magazine, 54: 695. 1876–77. P R
Liddon, Henry Parry. Dr. Liddon on the feminine ideal. Spectator, 58 (1): 541. 1885. P R
Comments on his protest, in a sermon, against imitation of masculine ideals by women.
Linton, Eliza Lynn. The future supremacy of women. National review, 8: 1. 1886. P R
Reprinted in the Eclectic, n. s., 44: 697 [P R].
Against the extension of the franchise to women, and, incidentally, against the higher education. Answered in the National review, 8: 408.
— The higher education of woman. Fortnightly review, 46: 498. 1886. P R
Reprinted in the Eclectic, n. s., 44: 812 [P R], and in the Popular science monthly, 30: 168 [P R]. Answered by Helen McKerlie in the Contemporary review, 51: 112. 1887 [P R].
— Woman's place in nature and society. Belgravia, 20: 349. 1876. P R
Reviewed in the Victoria magazine, 27: 244 [P R].

Livermore, Mary Ashton. What shall we do with our daughters? Superfluous women and other lectures. Boston, 1883. 3574.72
"Higher education," pp. 43–58.
Lohse, Johanne. Mistaken views on the education of girls. London, 1885.
Lord, John. The life of Emma Willard. N. Y., 1873. Portr. 2349.62
Lowe, Martha Perry. Some words about women. Old and new, 4: 287. 1871. P R
Lowell, Anna Cabot. Thoughts on the education of girls. Boston, 1853. 3599.31
Lumsden, Louisa Innes. On the higher education of women in Great Britain and Ireland. Journal of social science, 20: 49. 1885. P R
Machar, Agnes Maule. (Fidelis.) Higher education of women. Canadian monthly, 7: 144. 1875. P R
McKeen, Catharine. Mental education of women. American journal of education, 1: 567. 1856. P R
McKerlie, Helen. The lower education of women. Contemporary review, 51: 112. 1887. P R
In answer to Mrs. Lynn Linton's "Higher education of women."
Magnus, Lady Kate. The higher education of women. National review, 12: 663. 1889. P R
Reprinted in the Eclectic, n. s., 49: 246 [P R].
Manley, John Jackson. The higher education of women. British almanac and companion, 1882: 111. *2509.1 (1882)
Mann, Horace. A few thoughts on the powers and duties of woman. Two lectures. N. Y., 1859. No. 3 in *7589.86
Manning, E. A. Recent developments of education for the women and girls of India. (Proceedings of the International congress of education, Chicago, 1893, pp. 890–900.) *3592.145
Markby, Thomas. The education of women. Contemporary review, 1: 396; 7: 242. 1866, 1868. P R
Marsh, Charles Phelps. The education of women. Nation, 3: 165. 1866. P R
Marsh, Robert Winthrop. The higher education of women. [Descriptions mainly of Mt. Holyoke seminary and of Smith college.] Potter's American monthly, 10: 1. 1878. P R
Martin, H. B. The higher education of women. Catholic presbyterian, 4: 86. 1880.
Mater. In what degree may female talent be benefically cultivated? Christian observer, 7: 497. 1808. *7501.3.7
Mayor, Joseph Bickersteth. A conservative plea for the higher education of women. Victoria magazine, 23: 434. 1874. P R
— The cry of the women. Contemporary review, 11: 196. 1869. P R
Meriwether, Colyer. History of higher education in South Carolina. Washington, 1889. [U. S. Bureau of education. Circular of information, 1888, no. 3.] 3592.110
Education of women, pp. 103–108.
Merriam, Lucius Salisbury. Higher education in Tennessee. Washington, 1893. [U. S. Bureau of education. Circular of information, no. 5, 1893.] 7596.26
Colleges for women, pp. 245–260.
Meyer, Annie Nathan. The higher education for women in New York city. Nation, 46: 68. 1888. P R
Showing the need of an annex to Columbia college.

8

THE HIGHER EDUCATION OF WOMEN.

— editor. Woman's work in America. With
an introduction by Julia Ward Howe. N.Y.,
1891. 3575.119
Contains papers on the education of women in the
Eastern, Western, and Southern States with lists
of the coeducational colleges in these States, and
on woman in the learned professions. These papers
are entered under their several authors. There is
also appended a list of medical essays and communications written by women physicians between
1872 and 1890.
Middle-class education in England. Cornhill
magazine, 10: 549. 1864. P R
Miles, William Porcher. Women "nobly
planned." How to educate our girls. An
address delivered before the young ladies
of the Yorkville female college. [186–?]
No. 7 in *5574.29
Mitchell, Maria. The collegiate education of
girls: read at the congress of the Association for the advancement of women, 1880.
Education, 1: 433. 1881. P R
Monroe, H. E. Woman's educational movement in England. Education, 10: 489.
1891. P R
Monroe, Will S. The higher education of
women in Europe. Journal of education,
44: 12, 59. 1896. *7590.8.44
More, Hannah. Strictures on the modern
system of female education. London, 1799.
2 v.
— Same. Phila., 1800. 2 v. 3589.80
— Same. Charlestown, 1800. 3599.46
— Same. London, 1853. 2578.13.3
Morgan, L. D. Ladies and learning. Atlan-
tic monthly, 64: 518. 1889. P R
Mott, Lucretia. Discourse on woman, delivered at the Assembly buildings, Dec. 17,
1849. Phila., 1850. No. 8 in *5573.31
— Same. 1869. No. 14 in *7573.60
Movements for education of women. Unita-
rian review, 67: 217. 1876. P R
Mozzoni, Anna Maria. Un passo avanti nella
cultura femminile; tesi e progetto. Milano,
1866.
Notice of the founding of Vassar college, pp. 68–74.
Reviewed in the Nation, 3: 5 [P R].
National association for the promotion of social science. Report of a discussion on the
proposed admission of girls to university
local examinations. London, 1864.
No. 34 in *5566.6
Neal, J. A. An essay on the education and
genius of the female sex. Phila., 1795.
No. 2 in *5574.93
Newton, Richard Heber. The education of
our daughters. (Womanhood, pp. 275–315.
1881.) 3588.58
Novelties in female education. British quar-
terly review, 12: 193. 1850. P R
Nydegger, Louise. Russian women in Swiss
universities. Woman's journal, 24: 369, 378.
1893. *7260.51.24
Oakley, Henry Evelyn. Report [for 1894] on
the training colleges. [London, 1895. Great
Britain. Sessional papers.]
F.-R. Cr. 1895, vol. 28
Oertel, Hanns. Higher education in Ger-
many. Dial, 22: 75. 1897. P R
Comments on a pamphlet entitled Die akademische
Frau, by Arthur Kirchhoff.
Organ, J. P. Female adult education. Irish
quarterly review, 6: 165. 1856. P R
Orr, Alexandra. The future of English wom-
en. By Mrs. Sutherland Orr. Nineteenth
century, 3: 1010. 1879. P R

Orton, James, editor. The liberal education
of women; the demand and the method.
Current thoughts in America and England.
N. Y., 1873. *3598.54
Thirty-five papers by different authors.
O'Sullivan, B. A series of lectures on female
education. No. 1. Washington, 1828.
Ottmann, Rudolf. Beiträge zur Culturge-
schichte der polnischen Frauen im XVI.
und XVII. Jahrhunderte. Krakau, 1884.
5064.21
Oxford B.A., An. University degrees for
women. Fortnightly review, 63: 895. 1895.
P R
Oxford and Cambridge degrees for women.
British medical journal, 1896 (1): 417.
*7740.3.1896 (1)
Oxoniensis, pseud. The education of women.
Christian observer, 65: 542. 1865. P R
Remarks on Miss Cobbe's "Pursuits of women."
For comments on this article see page 794 of the
same volume.
— Further remarks on the education of wom-
en. Christian observer, 65: 870. 1865. P R
Palmer, Alice Freeman. The higher education
of women. Forum, 12: 28. 1891. P R
Pascoe, Charles Eyre. Schools for girls, and
colleges for women: a handbook of female
education, chiefly designed for the use of
persons of the upper middle class; together
with some chapters on the higher employ-
ment of women. London, 1879. 3597.68
Reviewed in Victoria magazine, 33: 168 [P R].
Patrick, Mary Mills. Education of women in
Turkey. Forum, 21: 440. 1896. P R
Peabody, Elizabeth Palmer. Female education
in Massachusetts. Reminiscences of subjects
and methods of teaching. Elizabeth P.
Peabody, Mrs. Palmer Peabody, Mrs. Mary
Peabody Mann. Hartford. [1880.] 3595.122
Reprinted from the American journal of education,
30: 584 [P R].
— The world's need of woman. Christian ex-
aminer, 69: 435. 1860. P R
Petersen-Studnitz, Alexis. Kvinde-kollegier
i Amerika. Nationaløkonomisk tidsskrift,
1887, 4e hefte.
Phelps, Almira. The female student; or lec-
tures to young ladies on female education.
N. Y., 1836. 5599.48
— The fireside friend, or female student: being
advice to young ladies on the important sub-
ject of education. Boston, 1840. [School
library.] 6245.11.18
Philbrick, John Dudley. Higher education of
girls in France. Journal of education, 22:
379. 1885. 7590.8.22
Pochhammer, Leo. Beitrag zur Frage des
Universitäts-Studium der Frauen. Kiel,
1893.
Porter, D. G. The liberal education of girls.
Christian quarterly, 5: 306. 1873. P R
Powell, Lyman P. History of education in
Delaware. Washington, 1893. [U. S. Bu-
reau of education. Circular of information,
no. 3, 1893.] 3592.138
Wesleyan female college, p. 83.
Powers of women and how to use them. Con-
temporary review, 14: 521. 1870. P R
Provisions for the liberal education of women.
Boston, 1876.
Reprinted from the Atlantic monthly, 38: 380 [P R].
Putnam, Alfred Porter. The education of
woman. Monthly religious magazine, 38:
252. 1867. *5397.1.38

Quilter, Harry. In the days of her youth. Nineteenth century, 37: 940. 1895. P R

Rambaud, Alfred. L'éducation des filles en Russie, et les gymnases des femmes. Revue des deux mondes, 2e pér., 104: 321. 1873. P R

Raymond, John Howard. The demand of the age for a liberal education for women, and how it should be met. (Proceedings of the National baptist educational convention, 1870, pp. 223-238.)

Reaney, Isabel. The higher education of women. Congregationalist, 7: 532. 1878.
*N.145.1.7

Remarks on female education. London, 1823.
3597.72

Remarks on the education of girls. London, 1854.

Rich, Ezekiel. A system of general education; ... designed especially, but not exclusively, for females of the middle and less opulent classes. Keene, N. H., 1835. No. 4 in *5595.6

Richardson, Charles Francis, and Henry Alden Clark. The college book. Boston, 1878.
*2382.2
Includes sketches of Wesleyan university, Oberlin, Michigan, Vassar, and Cornell, with those of the leading colleges which are exclusively for men.

Ridley, Annie E. Frances Mary Buss and her work for education. London, 1895. 3598.151
Reviewed in the Academy, 49: 400. 1896 [P R], and in the Critic, 26: 4 [P R].

Rockwell, Julius. Address, at the Pittsfield young ladies' institute, on the education of American women. Pittsfield, Mass., 1847.
No. 3 in *4392.76.1

Roscoe, ——. The nature and cause of the opposition to the movement on behalf of woman. Victoria magazine, 16: 101. 1870.
P R

Rousselot, Paul. Histoire de l'éducation des femmes en France. Paris, 1883. 2 v.
— La pédagogie féminine: extraite des principaux écrivains qui ont traité de l'éducation des femmes depuis le XVIe siècle. Paris, 1881.

Russell, Katharine Louisa, viscountess Amberley. Women's claims and men's monopolies. Victoria magazine, 16: 442. 1871.
P R

Russell, William. Female education. (Lectures before the American institute of instruction, 1844, pp. 33-62.) *3593.1 (1844)

Salmon, Lucy Maynard. History in college entrance examinations. Public opinion, 22: 87. 1897. P R
Condensed from the Journal of pedagogy.
— Unity of standard for college entrance examinations. Read before the Association of collegiate alumnæ. [Syracuse] Academy, 3: 222. 1888.

Sanborn, Edwin David. The progress of society as indicated by the condition of women. American biblical repository, 20: 91. 1842. P R

Sands, Alexander Hamilton. Intellectual culture of women. Southern literary messenger, 28: 321. 1859. P R

Santley, Herbert. Women. Lippincott's monthly magazine, 3: 432. 1869. P R

Scholarships open to women and girls in England. Nation, 46: 463. 1888. P R

Seelye, Laurenus Clark. Collegiate education of women. (Proceedings of the University convocation of the state of New York, 1879, pp. 91-97.) *6361.2 (1879)
— The higher education of women: its perils and its benefits. [Read before the American teachers' association at Newport, R. I., July 12, 1888.]
— The need of a collegiate education for woman. A paper read before the American institute of instruction, at North Adams. [Springfield, Mass.] 1874.

Sewall, May Wright. The education of woman in the Western states. (Meyer, Annie N., editor. Woman's work in America, pp. 84-88. 1891.) 3575.119
— Higher education for women in the United States. (Report of the International council of women, 1888, pp. 51-63.) *5586.65
Reprinted from the Woman's tribune, March 27, 1888.

Sewell, Elizabeth Missing. Principles of education, drawn from nature and revelation, and applied to female education in the upper classes. London, 1865. 2 v. 3599.38
— Same. N. Y., 1866. 3599.136
— The reign of pedantry in girls' schools. Nineteenth century, 23: 216. 1888. P R

Shirreff, Emily Anne E. College education for women. Contemporary review, 15: 55. 1870. P R
— Intellectual education, and its influence on the character and happiness of women. London, 1858.
— Same. New [2d] ed. 1862. 5598.61
— The kindergarten principles of Fröbel's system, and their bearing on the education of women. Also, remarks on the higher education of women. London, 1876. 3598.78

Should the education of women be the same as that of men? (Annual report of the Regents of the University of the state of New York, 1886, pp. 159-167.) *6461.1 (1886)
Discussion on a paper by T. J. Backus which is not published in the report.

Should university degrees be given to women? Westminster review, 115: 493. 1881. P R

Sidgwick, Mrs. Henry. The university education of women. (Proceedings of the International conference on education, 1884, pp. 364-374.) 3763.100.15

Sigourney, Lydia Huntley. Policy of elevating the standard of female education. Southern literary messenger, 1: 169. 1834.
P R

Sill, Edward Rowland. Shall women go to college? Century, 32: 323. 1886. P R
See brief replies in the same magazine, 33: 494; 34: 318 [P R].

Simcox, Edith J. Educational progress in England. Journal of social science, 12: 29. 1880. P R

Simms, Joseph. The past, present, and future of women. San Francisco, 1889. 3578.119

Sleyden, Henriette van der. Onderwijs, opvoeding en emancipatie der vrouwen. Door Marie Delsey [pseud.]. Delft, 1870.

Smedley, Menella Bute. The English girl's education. Contemporary review, 14: 29. 1870. P R

Smith, Annie Tolman. Progress of education for women. (U. S. Bureau of education. Annual report, 1871, pp. 511-518.)
*7595.1 (1871)

Smith, Charles Card. Self-culture of women. Christian examiner, 51: 185. 1851.   P R
Remarks on "Thoughts on self-culture, addressed to women," by Maria G. Grey.

Smith, Charles Forster. The higher education of women in the South. Educational review, 8: 287. 1894.   P R
Strictures on Miss Woodward's article entitled "Woman's education in the South."

Smith, Charles Lee. The history of education in North Carolina. Washington, 1888. [U.S. Bureau of education. Circular of information, no. 2, 1888.]   3596..101
"The higher female education," pp. 117-127.

Smith, Goldwin. University degrees for women. Saturday review, 81: 392. 1896.   P R

Smith, Norman H. Women's degrees at Oxford and Cambridge. Outlook, 53: 623. 1896.   P R

Smith, Sydney. Female education. Edinburgh review, 15: 273. 1810.   P R
A review of Thomas Broadhead's Advice to young ladies on the improvement of the mind. This may also be found in various editions of his Works.

Spalding, Helen F. Higher education of women. Portland, Oregon, 1883.

Spalding, James Reed. The true idea of female education. An address at Pittsfield, Mass., before the Young ladies' institute. N. Y., 1855.   No. 26 in *5590a.61

Special systems of education for women. Reprinted from the London student. [London, 1868.]   No. 12 in *5571.71

Stanley, Henrietta Maria Dillon, baroness. Personal recollections of women's education. Nineteenth century, 6: 308. 1879. P R

Stanton, Elizabeth Cady. Emma Willard, the pioneer in the higher education of women. Westminster review, 140: 538. 1893.   P R
— The woman question. The Radical, 3: 18. 1867.   *7302.2.3

Stanton, Theodore, editor. The woman question in Europe: a series of original essays. N. Y., 1884.   3572.53
Reviewed in Westminster review, 122: 185 [P R].

Steffens, J. B. Women at the university of Paris. Nation, 58: 151. 1894.   P R
— Women students and women teachers in Germany. Nation, 59: 232. 1894.   P R

Steinberg, Madame. Lectures on female education. Paris, 1855.

Steiner, Bernard Christian. History of education in Maryland. Washington, 1894. [U. S. Bureau of education. Circular of information, no. 2, 1894.]   3592.147
Woman's college of Baltimore, by John B. Van Nute, pp. 198-204; Baltimore female college, p. 269; Woman's medical college, by R. Winslow and J. T. Smith, pp. 300-303.

Stephens, Kate. Advanced education for women. Forum, 7: 41. 1889.   P R
— Position and education of American women. Encyclopædia Britannica, American reprint, 24: 908. 1889.

Stevens, Walter Le Conte. The admission of women to universities. Testimony gathered in connection with an essay on "University education for women." Published by the Association for promoting the higher education of women in New York. N. Y., 1883.   No. 10 in *5574.29
— University education for women. North American review, 136: 25. 1883.   P R

Stevenson, Louisa. Women students in the Scottish universities. [Slightly abridged.] (Proceedings of the International congress of education, Chicago, 1893, pp. 877-879.)   *3592.145

Stith, Mrs. Townshend. Thoughts on female education. Phila., 1831.   5594.22
Stoddard, Francis Hovey. Women in the English universities. New Englander, 45: 573. 1886.   P R

Stone, Andrew Leete. The mission of woman. An address at the fourteenth anniversary of the Mount Holyoke female seminary. Boston, 1851.   4498.153

Stone, Lucinda H. The influence of a foreign education on American girls. Education, 3: 14. 1882.   P R

Stowell, Louisa Reed. [Retrospect of educational opportunities for women.] (Report of the International council of women, 1888, pp. 72-75.)   *5586.65
Condensed from the Woman's tribune of March 27, 1888.

Strong, Augustus Hopkins. The education of a woman. (Philosophy and religion, pp. 418-430. 1888.)   3493.50
Suffrage and the higher education. Nation, 29: 364. 1879.   P R
Suppressed sex, The. Westminster review, 90: 437. 1868.   P R
Argues for higher education.

T., E. Female education. Southern literary messenger, 27: 218. 1858.   P R

Taylor, James Monroe. The future of the woman's college. An address on commencement day. (Addresses at the celebration of the completion of the 25th year of Vassar college, pp. 65-96. 1890.)   4496.209

Taylor, Whately Cooke. Strong-minded women. St. James's magazine, 15: 350 1866.

Ten Brook, Andrew. American state universities, their origin and progress. Cincinnati, 1875.
Discussion of the education of women, pp. 358-363.

Tetlow, John. The Eastern colleges for women: their aims, means, and methods. Education, 1: 465, 544. 1881.   P R
— Higher education of women. Educational review, 5: 388. 1893.   P R
— Some aspects of the higher education of women. [Boston, 1882.]   3597.122
Reprinted from the American institute of instruction, 1882, pp. 95-124 [*3593.1(1882)].

Thalheimer, Mary E. A letter on the education of girls. (Proceedings of the University convocation of the state of New York, 1867, pp. 33-41.)   *6361.2.4

Thorne, P. The coming woman. Lippincott's monthly magazine, 5: 529. 1870.   P R

Thwing, Charles Franklin. American colleges: their students and work. N. Y., 1878.   5599 67
— Same. 2d ed., revised and enlarged. 1883.
— The college and the home. Harper's bazar, 29: 490. 1896.   *5400.1.29
— College education of women. Outlook, 49: 729. 1894.   P R
— College education of young women. Harper's bazar, 26: 670, 715. 1893.   *5400.1.26
Reprinted, in an abridged form, in Public opinion, 16: 9 [P R].
— The college woman. N.Y. [1894.]   3597.131
— Recent movements in woman's education. Harper's New monthly magazine, 62: 101. 1880.   P R

11

Tod, Isabella M. S. Advanced education for girls of the upper and middle classes. (Transactions of the National association for the promotion of social science, 1868, pp. 368-378.) *5566.3 (1868)
— University examinations for women: a paper read before the Ladies' conference at the Social science congress at Newcastle-on-Tyne. Leisure hour, 20: 42. 1871. P R
Tolman, William Howe. The history of higher education in Rhode Island. [Washington.] 1894. 7592.16
Published by the Bureau of education as Circular of information, no. 1, 1894 [7596.56 (1894)]. Education of women, pp. 77-91.
Trasenster, Louis. L'enseignement supérieur pour les femmes. Discours inaugural. (Université de Liége. Année académique, 1882-83, pp. 3-51.) 5594.72
— L'instruction supérieure de la femme. Verviers, 1884.
Tyler, William Seymour. The higher education of women. An address before the trustees, teachers and pupils of Mount Holyoke seminary. With the address to the graduating class, by Rev. J. M. Greene. Northampton, Mass., 1874.
The address of Professor Tyler was reprinted in Scribner's monthly, 7: 456. 1873-74 [P R].
Tynan, Kate. The higher education of Catholic girls. Catholic world, 51: 616. 1890. P R
United States. Bureau of education. Account of college commencements during 1873 in the Western and Southern states. Washington, 1873. [Circular of information, no. 5, 1873.] *7596.59 (1873)
— Account of college commencements for the summer of 1873, in Maine, New Hampshire, Vermont, Massachusetts, Rhode Island, Connecticut, New York, New Jersey, and Pennsylvania. Washington, 1873. [Circular of information, no. 3, 1873.] *7596.59 (1873)
— High schools for girls in Sweden. Washington, 1882.
— Suggestions on the education of girls. Extracts from various authors. (Annual report, 1868, pp. 369-384.) *7505.1 (1868)
Most of the Commissioner's reports contain statistical tables of women's colleges.
University education for women [in Scotland]. Athenæum, 1892 (2): 590, 889. P R
University examinations for girls. Victoria magazine, 8: 73. 1866. P R
University women. Victoria magazine, 13: 289. 1869. P R
Viator, pseud. Female education in Italy. Nation, 3: 5. 1866. P R
Includes a review of Anna Mozzoni's "Passo avanti nella cultura femminile."
Villiers, Lady Margaret Elizabeth Leigh, countess of Jersey. Our grandmothers. National review, 8: 408. 1886. P R
Reprinted in Littell's living age, 171: 807 [P R]. A reply to Mrs. Lynn Linton's "Future supremacy of women."
W., E. E. Mental training of girls. St. James's magazine, 14: 361. 1865.
W., E. F. [Collegiate education for women.] Lippincott's monthly magazine, 39: 861. 1887. P R
Walker, Francis Amasa. Normal training in women's colleges. Educational review, 4: 328. 1892. P R

Wallington. Women as they are supposed to be and women as they are. Victoria magazine, 15: 395. 1870. P R
Watson, Georgianne E. Some defects in the higher education of women. (Papers read before the 5th congress of women, 1877, pp. 69-73.)
What women are educated for. Once a week, 5: 175. 1861. P R
Webster, Helen L. Woman's progress in higher education. (Transactions of the National council of women, 1891, pp. 192-199.) *5583.13
Wheeler, Emily F. Households of women. The Critic, n. s., 12: 89. 1889. P R
Criticising the "semiconventual" life in women's colleges.
Whibley, Charles. The encroachment of women. Nineteenth century, 38: 495. 1896. P R
Whitton, Frederick. Concerning accredited schools. Nation, 64: 29. 1897. P R
Wiese, Ludwig Adolf. Über weibliche Erziehung und Bildung: ein Vortrag. Berlin, 1865.
Wijck, Bernard Hendrik Cornelis Karel van der. De opvoeding der vrouw. Groningen, 1870.
Willard, Emma C. An address to the public, particularly to the members of the legislature of New York, proposing a plan for improving female education. Albany, 1819.
Reviewed in and extracted from the Phrenological journal, vol. 8.
— Advancement of female education, or a series of addresses in favor of establishing at Athens, in Greece, a female seminary. Troy [N. Y.], 1833. No. 14 in 75900.18
Wilson, D. [Higher education of women.] Canadian monthly, 12: 311. 1877. P R
In behalf of wider opportunities for women at the University of Toronto.
Winslow, Hubbard. The appropriate sphere of woman. A discourse delivered in the Bowdoin street church. Boston, 1837.
No. 1 in *5470a.87
— Woman as she should be. The appropriate sphere of woman. The influence of Christianity on woman. The Christian education of woman. By Hubbard Winslow. Also, Woman in her social and domestic character. By Mrs. John Sandford. From the 2d London ed. Boston, 1838. 5579.23
Republished, in great part, in 1854, in the Lady's manual [*7309.73].
Witte, A. On the education of girls. Education, 14: 229. 1893-94. P R
— The woman's educational movement in Germany. Education, 13: 37. 1892-93. P R
Wolkonsky, Serge, prince. Higher education of women in Russia. (U. S. Bureau of education. Report of the commissioner for 1892-93, vol. 1, pp. 687-690.) *7595.1 (1892/93) vol. 1
Wolstenholme, Elizabeth C. The education of girls, its present and its future. (Butler, Josephine E., editor. Woman's work and woman's culture, pp. 290-330. 1869.) 5573.34
Woman. Dial, 1: 362. 1841. *5235.4.1
Woman. Littell's living age, 59: 483. 1858. P R

Woman, her position, influence, and wishes. National review, 7: 333. 1858. P R Reprinted in the Eclectic magazine, 46: 1. 1859 [P R].

Woman question, The. Canadian monthly, 15: 568. 1879. P R

Women and the universities. Spectator, 60: 855. 1887. P R

Women at Cambridge and Oxford. Nation, 45: 30. 1887. P R

Women's education. Fraser's magazine, 79: 537. 1869. P R

Woodbridge, William. Female education prior to 1800. Barnard's journal of education, 27: 273. 1877. P R

Woodward, Mary V. Higher education of women in the South. Educational review, 9: 187. 1895. P R
An answer to C. F. Smith's strictures on the following article.

— Woman's education in the South. Educational review, 7: 466. 1893. P R

Wordsworth, E. Colleges for women. (Ladies at work, pp. 14–28. 1893.) 3574.112

Working women's college. Victoria magazine, 8: 97. 1866. P R

Zévort, Charles Marie. Higher education in France. Address to the French minister of public instruction, at the inauguration of the Girls' high school in Le Havre. Trans. by Margaret K. Smith. Journal of education, 22: 323. 1885. *7590.8.22

Zimmern, Alice. Women at the German universities. Athenæum, 1895 (1): 642. P R

— Women in European universities. Forum, 19: 1ᵠ7. 1895. P R

II.   Higher Education in Relation to Health.

This includes physical education and the question of the mental inferiority of women.

Allen, Grant. Plain words on the woman question. Popular science monthly, 36: 170. 1889. P R
"We will not aid or abet woman as a sex in rebelling against maternity," p. 181.

Allen, Mary E. Physical development of women and children. (Proceedings of the American association for the advancement of physical education, 1890, pp. 9–21.) 8006.1 (1890)

Allen, Nathan. The education of girls, as connected with their growth and physical development. Sanitarian, 7: 385. 1879. *5760a.50.7

American women: their health and education. Westminster review, 102: 456. 1874. P R
Reviews Dr. Clarke's "Sex in education" with "The education of American girls," edited by A. C. Brackett.

Anderson, Elizabeth Garrett. Sex in mind and education: a reply [to Dr. Maudsley]. Fortnightly review, 21: 582. 1874. P R

Association of collegiate alumnæ. Health statistics of women college graduates. Report of a special committee, Annie G. Howes, chairman. Boston, 1885.
Reviewed in the Nation, 41: 295, under the heading, "The health of American women;" in the Christian register, Oct. 29, 1895, "The health of college girls;" by John Dewey in Science, 6: 341; and in the Popular science monthly, 28: 606.

— Physical education for scholastic women. (Hartwell, E. M. Physical training in American colleges, pp. 132–134. 1886.) *7596.59 (1885)

At the parting of the ways. Atlantic monthly, 76: 691. 1895. P R

Basket-ball on the Pacific coast. Harper's bazar, 29: 469. 1896. *5400.1.29

Batten, Rayner Winterbotham. An address on the physical training of girls. British medical journal, 1887 (1): 605. *7740.3.1887 (1)

Becker, Lydia E. On some supposed differences in the minds of men and women with reference to educational necessities. A paper read in section F of the British association at Norwich, 1868.
An abstract of this paper was published in the Report of the Association, pp. 155, 156 [*791a.1. 1868].

Benneson, Cora Agnes. Health of college women. New England kitchen magazine, 3: 66. 1895.
Extracts from an article on the College education of women, originally published in the Journal of pedagogy, 8: 13. 1894.

Bissell, Mary Taylor. Emotions versus health in women. Popular science monthly, 32: 504. 1888. P R

— Physical development and exercise for women. N. Y., 1891. Illus. [Portia series.] 4009.164

— Same. 1893. 4009a.159

— Physical training as a factor in liberal education. A paper presented to the Association of collegiate alumnæ. 1886.

— The physical training of women. (Proceedings of the American association for the advancement of physical education, 1888, pp. 8–17.) *8006.1.4

Blackwell, Antoinette Brown. Comparative mental power of the sexes physiologically considered. (Papers read before the Congress of women, 1877, pp. 19–26.)
Reprinted in the Victoria magazine, 28: 405 [P R].

— The sexes throughout nature. N. Y., 1875. 3578.61
In reply to Dr. Clarke's "Sex in education."

Bonavia, E. The struggle of the sexes. Free review, 3: 75. 1894. *5403 6.3
A review of Dr. Strahan's article in vol. 3 of the Humanitarian.

Brainerd, Adelia K. [Athletics in women's colleges.] Harper's bazar, 30: 59. 1897. *5400.1.30

Brooks, William Keith. The evidence from the intellectual differences between men and women. (Law of heredity, pp. 242-274. 1883.) 3824.72
First printed in the Popular science monthly, 15: 145, 347 (1879), under the title "The condition of women from a zoological point of view."
— Woman from the standpoint of a naturalist. Forum, 22: 286. 1896-97. P R

Brown, E. The education of women, physical and mental. Victoria magazine, 11: 384. 1868. P R

Browne, Sir James Crichton. Sex in education. British medical journal, 1892 (1): 949. *7740.3.1892 (1)
See also the author's replies to comments on this article on pp. 1046, 1110, 1227, 1329 of the same volume. Largely reprinted in the Educational review, 4: 164 [P R].

Bruehl, Carl Bernhard. "Einiges über die Gaben der Natur an die Frau, und die Consequenzen hieraus für Bedeutung, Stellung, Aufgaben und Rechte der Frau in der menschlichen Gesellschaft," eine von Gehirn-Demonstrationen begleiteter Vortrag. Wien. 1893.
Aus Jahresbericht des Vereines für erweiterte Frauenbildung in Wien.

Bryan, Mrs. R. S. Physical education in women's colleges. Journal of social science, 20: 45. 1885. P R

Buck, Gertrude, editor. Athletic education for women. A symposium. The Inlander, 6: 291. 1896.

Buechner, Friedrich Carl Christian Ludwig. Brain of women. New review, 9: 166. 1893. P R
Same article in Eclectic magazine, 58: 404 [P R].

Chatterton, Richard. On the difference between the sexes. Portfolio, 32: 25. 1824. *3200.20.32

Chreiman, M. A. Physical culture of women. Journal of the society of arts, 36: 647. 1887-88. *4012.375.36
— Physical education of girls. Health exhibition literature, 12: 203. 1884. 3763.100.12

Clarke, Edward Hammond. The building of a brain. (Addresses and proceedings of the National educational association, 1874, pp. 100-109.) 3596.50 (1874)
— Same. Enlarged. Boston, 1874. 3768.62
Contents: Nature's working plans. — An error in female building. — A glimpse at English brain-building.
— Sex in education; or, a fair chance for the girls. Boston, 1873. 3779.63
Reviewed in the Unitarian review, 1: 163. 1874; also in Monthly religious magazine, 50: 552, 1873 ['5397.1.50].
See also answers in this same section by Antoinette Blackwell, G. F. Comfort and Anna Manning, Eliza B. Duffey, W. B. Greene, Julia Ward Howe, and others.

Clegg, Joseph T. Some of the ailments of woman due to her higher development in the scale of evolution. Texas health journal, 3: 57. 1890-91.

Clouston, Thomas Smith. Female education from a medical point of view; being two lectures delivered at the Philosophical institution, Edinburgh. Edinburgh, 1882.
The first of these lectures may be found also in the Popular science monthly, 21: 214, 1883-84; the second in the same volume, p. 319.

Comfort, George Fisk, and Anna Manning. Woman's education, and woman's health: chiefly in reply to "Sex in education." Syracuse, 1874. 3779.66

Cook, Charles Henry. The effects of college life at Wellesley. [Read June 13, 1893.] Massachusetts medical society, Medical communications, 16: 190. 1895. *7737.10.16

Cummings, Elizabeth. Education as an aid to the health of women. Popular science monthly, 17: 823. 1880. P R

Delines, Michel. La capacité intellectuelle de la femme. Revue encyclopédique Larousse, 7: 12. 1897. *4690.50.7
Translated in the Scientific American supplement, 43: 17611 [P R].

Dewey, John. Education and health of women. Science, 6: 341. 1885. P R
— Health and sex in higher education. Popular science monthly, 28: 606. 1886. P R

Due, Malvern Nicholas. On the physical education of the fair sex. Alabama medical and surgical age, 2: 419. 1889-90.

Duffey, Eliza Bisbee. No sex in education; or, an equal chance for both girls and boys. Being a review of Dr. Clarke's "Sex in education." Phila., 1874. 3598.60

Educated to death: a mother's story. Popular science monthly, 6: 57. 1874. P R
Reprinted from Dr. Clarke's "Building of a brain."

Effect of college life on the health of women. New York medical journal, 37: 632. 1883. *7775.1.37

Ellis, Havelock. Man and woman: a study of human secondary sexual characters. London. [1894. Contemporary science series.] 3828.102

Feminine athletics. Victoria magazine, 33: 456. 1879. P R

French, Anna D. The comparative effects on health of professional, fashionable, and industrial life. (Papers read before the Association for the advancement of women, 1886, pp. 51-61.) *7572.70 (1886)

G., A. M. The intellectuality of woman. International review, 13: 123. 1882. P R

Gardener, Helen H. More about men's and women's brains. Popular science monthly, 31: 698. 1887. P R
— Sex and brain-weight. Popular science monthly, 31: 266. 1887. P R
— Sex in brain. (Report of the International council of women, 1888, pp. 369-382.) *5586.65
Disproves some of the statements of Dr. Hammond. Reprinted from the Woman's tribune. April 3.

Garnett, Lucy Mary Jane. The fallacy of the equality of woman. Woman's world, 1: 529. 1888.
In reply to Mrs. Laura M'Laren, The fallacy of the superiority of man, in the January number of the same magazine.

Greene, William Batchelder. Critical comments upon certain special passages in the introductory portion of Dr. Clarke's book on "Sex in education." Boston, 1874.
No. 4 in 7598.20

Grelley, —. Éducation physique de la femme. Pratique médicale, 4: 173. 1890.

Hall, Lucy Mabel. Physical training of girls. Popular science monthly, 26: 495. 1885. P R
— Physical training of women. Journal of social science, 21: 100. 1886. P R

Hammond, William Alexander. Men's and women's brains. Popular science monthly, 31: 554. 1887. P R

Hardaker, M. A. The ethics of sex. North American review, 131: 62. 1880. P R

Hartwell, Edward Mussey. Physical training in American colleges and universities. Washington, 1886. [U. S. Bureau of education. Circular of information, no. 5, 1885.]
*7506.59 (1885)
— The rise of college gymnasiums in the United States. (Proceedings of the International conference on education, 1884, pp. 357–394.)   3763.100.13

Hayes, Alice. Health of women students in England. Education, 11: 284. 1890–91. P R

Health and fertility of educated women. Medical record, 28: 407. 1885.   *7741.1.28
A review of the Association of collegiate alumnæ health statistics.

Health of American women. Nation, 41: 295. 1885.   P R

Health of the graduates of women's colleges. Medical news, 42: 680. 1883.   *7715.1.42

Howe, Julia Ward, editor. Sex and education. Boston, 1874.
"Contains the views of a number of thoughtful persons, chiefly women, upon the matters treated of in Dr. Clarke's work entitled 'Sex in education,' and upon the book itself." — Introduction.

Huling, Ray Greene. College women and physical training. Educational review, 7: 78. 1894.   P R

Is there such a thing as sex? Nation, 8: 87. 1869.   P R

Jenks, Edward W. The education of girls from a medical standpoint. Transactions of the Michigan medical society, 13: 52. 1889.

Le Bon, Gustave. La psychologie des femmes et les effets de leur éducation actuelle. Revue scientifique, 46: 449. 1890. *5292.1.46
There is an abstract of this in the Educational review, 1: 101. 1891 [P R].

Livermore, Daniel Parker. Woman's mental status. Forum, 5: 90. 1888.   P R

McLaren, Agnes. Physical exercise for women. Northwestern lancet, 8: 20. 1888.

M'Laren, Laura. The fallacy of the superiority of man. Woman's world, 1: 54. 1888.
Reviewed by Miss L. M. J. Garnett in the same magazine, November, 1888.

Marvel, Louis H. How does college life affect the health of women? Education, 3: 501. 1883.   P R
Favorable testimonies from various college presidents and others.

Maudsley, Henry. Sex in mind and education. Fortnightly review, 21: 466. 1874.   P R
Reprinted in the Popular science monthly, 5: 198 [P R].

Mitchell, Silas Weir. [Values and perils of the higher education.] (Doctor and patient, pp. 148–154. 1888.)   5767.78

Moore, William Withers. President's address at the annual meeting of the British medical association. British medical journal, 1886 (2): 295.   *7740.3.1886 (2)
Also published in the Times, Aug. 11, 1886. An editorial upon this address appears in the same number of the Times. The address is reviewed in the Spectator, 59: 1076 [P R], and in the Popular science monthly, 30: 612. 1887 [P R].

Morais, Nina. The limitations of sex. North American review, 132: 79. 1881.   P R
A review of Miss Hardaker's "Ethics of sex."

On Dr. Clarke's "Sex in education." North American review, 118: 140. 1874.   P R

Orme, Eliza. Woman's work in creation. Longman's magazine, 9: 149. 1886. P R
A reply to Dr. B. W. Richardson.

Osgood, Hamilton. The need of a radical change in the education and training of the

American girl, and the physician's duty therein. Boston medical and surgical journal, 104: 289. 1881.   5746.1.104
From advance sheets of the College and clinical record.

Parvin, Theophilus. Woman and her physician: a lecture delivered in the medical department of the University of Louisville. Louisville, Ky., 1870.

Patrick, George Thomas White. The psychology of woman. Popular science monthly, 47: 209. 1895.   P R
"If superiority consists in adaptation to present environment, then man is superior; if it consists in the possession of those underlying qualities which are essential to the race, then woman is superior."

Payne, Robert L. The health of our school-girls. North Carolina medical journal, 12: 121. 1883.

Perrigo, James. Overstudy in young ladies' schools and convents. Canada medical record, 8: 4. 1879–80.

Pfeiffer, Emily. Women and work. An essay treating on the relation to health and physical development of the higher education of girls, and the intellectual or more systematized effort of women. Boston, 1887.
— Same. London, 1888.   5575.94
Reviewed in the Spectator, 61: 210.

Physical education of female college students. Medical news, 41: 437. 1882.   *7715.1.41

Porter, Charlotte W. Physical hindrances to teaching girls. Forum, 12: 41. 1891.   P R

Preston, Grace A. The influence of college life on the health of women. [Read June 13, 1893.] Massachusetts medical society. Medical communications, 16: 167. 1895.
*7737.10.16

Read, Elizabeth Fisher. Basket-ball at Smith college. Outlook, 54: 557. 1896.   P R

Richards, Ellen Henrietta, and Marion Talbot. Food as a factor in student life. Chicago, 1894. [University of Chicago. Department of social science.]   3762.133

Richardson, Benjamin Ward. Woman's work in creation. Longman's magazine, 8: 604. 1886.   P R
See the reply of Miss Orme in December number of Longman's.

Richardson, Sophia Foster. Tendencies in athletics for women in colleges and universities. A paper presented to the Association of collegiate alumnæ, Oct. 31, 1896. [N. Y., 1897.]
Reprinted from Appleton's Popular science monthly, 50: 517. 1897 [P R].

Romanes, George John. Concerning woman. Forum, 4: 509. 1887–88.   P R
— Mental differences between men and women. Nineteenth century, 21: 654. 1887. P R
Reprinted in the Popular science monthly, 31: 383.

Scoville, S., jr. Athletic Vassar. Outlook, 54: 17. 1896.   P R

Sidgwick, Mrs. Henry. Health statistics of women students of Cambridge and Oxford, and of their sisters. Cambridge, 1890.

Simcox, Edith. The capacity of women. Nineteenth century, 22: 391. 1887.   P R
In reply to "Mental differences between men and women," by G. J. Romanes.

Skene, Alexander Johnston Chalmers. Education and culture as related to the health and diseases of women. Detroit, 1889.

Thorburn, John. Female education from a physiological point of view. A lecture, introductory to the summer course on obstetric medicine. Manchester, 1884. 5598.81

Tweedy, Alice B. Is education opposed to motherhood? Popular science monthly, 36: 751. 1890. P R

Van de Warker, Ely. The genesis of woman. Popular science monthly, 5: 269. 1874. P R

— The relations of women to the professions and skilled labor. Popular science monthly, 6: 454. 1875. P R
Argues, on physiological grounds, against successful competition with men. Reviewed by Frances E. White in Penn monthly, 6: 514 [P R].

Van Rensselaer, Mariana Griswold. Waste of women's intellectual force. Forum, 13: 616. 1892. P R

White, Frances Emily. Dr. Van de Warker on "The relations of women to the professions and skilled labor." Penn monthly, 6: 514. 1875. P R

Winsor, Frederick. School hygiene. (Fifth annual report of the Massachusetts State board of health, pp. 391-448. 1874.) *6457.16 (1874)

Wright, Carroll Davidson. Health statistics of female college graduates. Boston, 1885. 3765.104
Reprinted from the Annual report of the Massachusetts Bureau of statistics of labor [*6443.3(1885)].

III.   Coeducation.

Allen, William Francis. The sexes in colleges. Nation, 10: 134. 1870. P R

Barnard, Frederick Augstus Porter. Should American colleges be open to women as well as to men? A paper presented to the twentieth annual convocation of the University of the state of New York. Albany, 1882.
Reprinted from the Proceedings of the convocation, pp. 141-160 [*6361.2. 1882].

Barney, Elizabeth Cynthia. Co-education at University college, London. Harper's bazar, 30: 90. 1897. *5400.1.30

Beedy, Mary E. The joint education of young men and women in the American schools and colleges. London, 1873. 7594.16

Blake, Sophia Jex. A visit to some American schools and colleges [including Oberlin, Hillsdale, and Antioch, with remarks on coeducation]. London, 1867. 3598.65

Bolton, Sarah Knowles. Women in the same college with men [Adelbert college]. Journal of education, 20: 379. 1884. *7590.8.20

Boston. School committee. Majority and minority reports of the special committee on the subject of co-education of the sexes. Boston, 1890. [School document no. 19.]

Brackett, Anna Callender. Coeducation at Cornell. New England journal of education, 7: 137. 1878. *7590.8.7
Reprinted in Victoria magazine, 31: 218.

— Over a new road [to coeducation]. Education, 1: 156. 1880. P R

Bridges, Flora. Coeducation in Swiss universities. Popular science monthly, 38: 524. 1890-91. P R

Brons, Bernhard. Ueber die gemeinsame Erziehung beider Geschlechter an den höheren Schulen. Mit Rücksicht auf thatsächliche Verhältnisse, hauptsächlich in den Vereinigten Staaten. Skandinavien und Finland. Hamburg, 1889. [Deutsche Zeit- und Streit-Fragen.] No. 11 in *5216.50.N.F.3

Burgon, John William. To educate young women like young men, and with young men, a thing inexpedient and immodest. A sermon preached before the University of Oxford in the chapel of New College, Oxford. [1884.]

Campbell, Dudley. Mixed education of boys and girls in England and America. London, 1874. No. 6 in *7592.6

Coeducation at Antioch college. Nation, 11: 24. 1870.

Coeducation in American colleges. Critic, 3: 153. 1883.

Coeducation in German universities. Nation, 55: 42. 1892. P R

Coeducation question. Nation, 16: 349. 1873. P R

Crow, Martha Foote. Will the coeducated coeducate their children? Forum, 17: 582. 1894. P R

Deems, Charles Force. The progress of coeducation. Forum, 3: 631. 1887. P R

Education and coeducation [for girls]. Critic, 11: 85. 1887.

Education of women in America. Westminster review, 100: 320. 1873. P R
Deals with facts, and favors coeducation.

Fairchild, James Harris. Coeducation at Oberlin. Bibliotheca sacra, 46: 443. 1889. P R

— Coeducation of the sexes; an address before a meeting of college presidents at Springfield, Ill., July 10, 1867. (U. S. Bureau of education. Annual report, 1868, pp. 385-400.) *7595.1.1868
Also in American journal of education, 17: 385.

Frazer, Persifor. Coeducation. Phila., 1890. 3596.115

Gilman, Arthur. The proper education of girls. Nation, 64: 47. 1897. P R

Godkin, Edwin Lawrence. The coeducation question. Nation, 16: 349. 1873. P R

Goodell, William, and others. Coeducation and the higher education of women. A symposium. Medical news, 55: 67. 1889. *7715.1.55
Reviewed in the New England medical gazette, 25: 58. 1890 [*7804.1.25], under the title, "Higher education again."

Gould, Elizabeth Porter. The woman problem. Education, 12: 73. 1891-92. P R

Grant, Sir Alexander, bart. Education and coeducation. Canadian monthly, 16: 500. 1879. P R

Hawtrey, Mabel. The coeducation of the sexes. London, 1896. 3599.155

Higginson, Thomas Wentworth. Women and men. The undergraduate point of view.

Harper's bazar, 21: 130. 1888.   *5400.1.21
Also in the Woman's journal, March 3, 1888.
Hopkins, Louisa Parsons. Coeducation in the public schools of Boston. Educational review, 1: 46. 1891.   P R
Hosmer, James Kendall. Coeducation of the sexes in universities. (Addresses and proceedings of the National educational association, 1874, pp. 118–133.)   *3596.50.1874
Jacobi, Mary Putnam. The higher education of women. Medical news, 56: 75. 1890.   *7715.1.56
M. Adelbert college, or coeducation. Nation, 53: 142. 1891.   P R
Magill, Helen. An address upon the coeducation of the sexes. Phila., 1873.
— Coeducation of the sexes in Swarthmore college. Phila., 1874.
Merrill. William A. The progress of coeducation. Nation, 46: 52. 1888.   P R
Answered on pages 91 and 116 of the same volume, by Christine Ladd Franklin and others.
Michaels, Rena A. Coeducation. (Report of the International council of women, 1888, pp. 75–77.)   *5586.65
Reprinted from the Woman's tribune, March 28, 1888.
Palmer, Minerva. Coeducation and the higher education of women. Medical news, 56: 77. 1890.   *7715.1.56
Pickard, Josiah Little. Coeducation in colleges. Education, 13: 259. 1892–3.   P R
Sarcey, Francisque. Coeducation. Cosmopolitan, 19: 354. 1894.   P R
Scott, Fred N. An Americanism. [History of the word coeducation.] Nation, 58: 48. 1894.   P R
Sewall, May Wright. Coeducation in secondary schools and colleges. Arena, 17: 767. 1897.   P R

Sexes, The, in colleges. Nation, 10: 134. 1870.   P R
Stone, Lucinda H. Coeducation in the University of Michigan. Boston evening transcript, Aug. 14, 1885.
Reprinted in the Woman's journal, Sept. 12.
Tarbell, H. S. Coeducation. Education, 4: 427. 1884.   P R
Thwing, Charles Franklin. Women's education. Education, 4: 53. 1883.   P R
An argument based upon the facts of experience, for coeducation.
United States. Bureau of education. Coeducation of the sexes in the public schools of the United States. Washington, 1883. [Circular of information, no. 2.] *7596.59 (1883)
Voss, P. Coeducation of the sexes. Substance of an address before the sixth Scandinavian school conference in Copenhagen, August. 1890. (U. S. Bureau of education. Annual report of the commissioner for 1888–89, vol. 1, pp. 464–469.) *7595.1 (1888/89), vol. 1
Walker, Marie Louise Hall. Early days of coeducation. The Inlander, 6: 276. 1896.
Wallington, ——. Advantages possessed by the system of mixed education over the separate system. Victoria magazine, 18: 487. 1872.   P R
Warren, William Fairfield. Argument on the admission of girls to the Boston Latin school. [Boston, 1887.] No. 7 in *7594.11
Wayland, Heman Lincoln. The question of the education of the women of the West, including that of the admission of both sexes to the same institutions of higher learning. (Proceedings of the Western Baptist educational convention, 1871, pp. 18–29, 85–86.)

IV.   Professional and Scientific Education.

Chauvin, Jeanne. Étude historique sur les professions accessibles aux femmes. Paris, 1892.
Reviewed by Alfred Berlyn in the Westminster review, 139: 381. 1893 [P R].
Future of women in professions. Public opinion, 70: 472. 1896.   P R
Tetlow, John. The education of women for the learned professions. Educational review, 11: 105. 1896.   P R
Women in the learned professions. Public opinion, 14: 401. 1892–3.
From the San Francisco examiner.

Law.

Bittenbender, Ada M. Women in law. (Report of the International council of women, 1888, pp. 173–179.)   5586.65
Reprinted from the Woman's tribune, March 30.
— Same. (Meyer, Annie N., editor. Woman's work in America, pp. 218–244. 1891.)   3575.119
Boston university. School of law. Catalogue, 1873/74–95/96, and circular, 1873/74–96/97. Boston, 1874–96.   4492.109

— Law student, The. Vol. 1. Boston, 1897.
Cornell university. Department of law. Announcement, 1887–96. Ithaca, 1887–95.
— Announcement of the summer term, 1893–95: Ithaca, 1893–95.
Goodell, Lavinia. Women in the legal profession. (Papers read before the Congress of women, 1877, pp. 103–113.)
Reprinted in the Victoria magazine, 29: 124.
Green, Mary A. Women in the law. Woman's journal, 22: 56. 1891.   *7260.51.22
Kilgore, Carrie Burnham. Address before the legislature of Pennsylvania, delivered in the hall of the House of representatives. Phila., 1881.   No. 8 in *5572.97
In support of a bill providing that no person shall be refused admission as attorney in Pennsylvania on account of sex.
King, Richard. Women in the legal profession. Victoria magaine, 28: 217. 1877. P R
Miller, Joseph Dana. Women at the bar. Demorest's family magazine, 33: 16. 1896.
Robinson, Lelia Josephine. Women lawyers in the United States. Green bag, 2: 10. 1890.   P R
Strickland, Martha. Woman and the forum. Green bag, 3: 240. 1891.   P R

Women as lawyers. Lippincott's monthly magazine, 23: 387. 1879.   P R

Women lawyers. Leslie's illustrated weekly, 83: 363. 1896.   *6941.15.83

Medicine.

A., M. E. The Woman's medical college of Pennsylvania. Vassar miscellany, 12: 249. 1883.

Abramoff, J. [The medical course of lectures for women.] St. Petersburg, 1886.
In Russian.

Admission of women to medical degrees by the University of London. Victoria magazine, 28: 514. 1877.   P R

Admission of women to the [British medical] association. British medical journal, 1892 (2): 383, 420.   *7740.3.1892 (2)

Admission of women to the Oxford medical examinations. British medical journal, 1891 (1): 188.   *7740.3.1891 (1)

American medical association. The discussion on the female physician question [in convention at San Francisco]. Boston medical and surgical journal, n. s., 7: 350, 371. 1871.   *5746.1.7, n.s.

Anderson, Elizabeth Garrett. The history of a movement. Fortnightly review, 59: 404. 1893.   P R

— The medical woman's movement in Great Britain and Ireland to Jan., 1893. (World's congress of representative women, pp. 209–214. 1894.)   5583.14

An appeal in behalf of the medical education of women. N. Y., 1856. No. 1 in *5771.56
An appeal for a woman's hospital connected with the New York infirmary for women.

Ashby, Thomas A. Abstract of an address on the medical education of women, delivered at the opening of the first course of lectures of the Women's medical college of Baltimore. Maryland medical journal. 9: 267. 1882–83.   *7792.60.9

Association for the advancement of the medical education of women. Report of the association, with addresses delivered at Union League hall. N. Y., 1878.

August, Otto. Die Krankenpflege durch Frauen mit Rücksicht auf gegenwärtige Verhältnisse. Wien, 1872.

B., C. Public demands and the medical education of women. Nation, 50: 237. 1890. P R

Baker, Paul De Lacy. The annual oration. Shall women be admitted into the medical profession? (Transactions of the Medical association of the state of Alabama, 1880, pp. 191–206.)   *7773.4 (1880)

Baudouin, M. Medical ladies abroad and at home. Providence medical journal, 13: 352. 1894.

Bischoff, Theodor Ludwig Wilhelm von. Das Studium und die Ausübung der Medicin durch Frauen. München, 1872.
Reprinted from the Allgemeine Zeitung, 1872 (3): 3567, 3584; 1872 (4): 4622 [6300.2].

Blackwell, Elizabeth. Address on the medical education of women, Dec. 27, 1855. N. Y., 1856.

— Medicine as a profession for woman. Victoria magazine, 15: 121. 1870.   P R

— Pioneer work in opening the medical profession to women. Autobiographical sketches. London, 1895.   4549a.142
Reviewed in the Nation, 62: 364. 1896.

— and Emily Blackwell. Address on the medical education of women [before a meeting at the New York infirmary. Dec. 19, 1863]. N. Y., 1864.   No. 3 in *5771.56

— — Medicine as a profession for women. N. Y., 1860.   No. 2 in *5771.56
Also in the English woman's journal, 5: 145.

Blackwood, Harriot Georgina, marchioness of Dufferin and Ava. A record of three years' work of the National association for supplying female medical aid to the women of India. Calcutta, 1888.

Blake, Sophia Jex. The medical education of women. (Transactions of the National association for the promotion of social science, 1873, pp. 385–393.)   *5566.3 (1873)

— Same. London. 1874.

— The medical education of women. Medical magazine, 1: 1138. London, 1892–3.
Also in the Woman's medical journal, 1: 105. Toledo, 1893.

— The medical education of women in Great Britain and Ireland. (World's congress of representative women, 1894, pp. 214–221.   5583.14

— Medical women. Edinburgh, 1872.   3576.88
Reviewed under the heading Women and medicine, in the Saturday review, 34: 641.

— Same. [2d ed.] 1886.   3576.37

— Same. Reprinted. Published by the National association for promoting the medical education of women. 1888.

— Same. Revised. 1896.

— Medical women. Nineteenth century, 22: 692. 1887.   P R

— Medical women in fiction. Nineteenth century, 33: 261. 1893.   P R

— Medicine as a profession for women. (Butler, Josephine E., editor. Woman's work and woman's culture, pp. 78–120. 1869.)   5573.34

— The practice of medicine by women. Edinburgh, 1876.
Reprinted from the Fortnightly review, 23: 392. 1875. "A statement of facts and conditions, legal and professional, which practically exclude women from the authorized practice of medicine" in England.

Bodley, Rachel Littler. Introductory lecture at the opening of the twenty-sixth annual session of the Woman's medical college of Pennsylvania. Phila., 1875.   7739.64

— Valedictory address to the twenty-second graduating class of the Woman's medical college of Pennsylvania. Phila., 1874. 7736.72

— Valedictory address to the twenty-ninth graduating class of the Woman's medical college of Pennsylvania. Phila., 1881. 7731.50
The title on the cover is The college story.
Reviewed under the title, "Women as physicians," in the Medical and surgical reporter, 44: 354.

Böhmert, Karl Victor. Das Studieren der Frauen mit besonderer Rücksicht auf das Studium der Medicin. Leipzig, 1872.
First printed anonymously in the supplements of the Allgemeine Zeitung, 1872(3): 3149, 3182, 3198. See letter of Dr. Böhmert on page 4036 of the same volume.

Bolton, Henry Carrington. The early practice of medicine by women. Popular science monthly, 18: 191. 1880.   P R
Reprinted in the Journal of science, 18: 57. 1881.

— Same. London, 1881.   No. 4 in *5771.56
Bolton, Sarah Knowles. Rachel Littler Bodley. (Successful women, pp. 149–174. 1888.)
1554.16
Boston university. School of medicine. Annual announcement and catalogue, 1873/74–96/97. Boston, 1873–96.   *4393.69
— Medical student. [Monthly.] Vol. 1–9. Boston, 1888–97.
— What it is doing and what it needs. [Boston, 1887.]   7739.102
Bowditch, Henry Ingersoll. The medical education of women. Boston medical and surgical journal, 101: 67. 1879.   *5746.1.101
— The medical education of women. The present hostile position of Harvard university and of the Massachusette medical society. What remedies therefor can be suggested? [Boston, 1881.]
Reprinted from the Boston medical and surgical journal, 105: 289 [*5746.1.105].
Brown, William Symington. The capability of women to practice the healing art; a lecture before the Ladies' medical academy. Boston, 1859.   No. 5 in *5792.74
Bryant, Emily J. The Woman's medical college of Pennsylvania. Education, 11: 12. 1890–91.   P R
Byford, William Heath. An address introductory to the course of instruction in the Woman's hospital medical college. Chicago. [1870.]
— Doctorate address delivered at the commencement of the Women's medical college. Chicago medical journal and examiner, 48: 561. 1884.
On woman's fitness for the practice of medicine.
Chadwick, James Read. The admission of women to the Massachusetts medical society. Boston, 1882.   7737.15
Reprinted from the Boston medical and surgical journal, 106: 547 [*5746.1.106].
— The study and practice of medicine by women. N. Y. [1879.]   No. 5 in *5771.56
Reprinted from the International review, 7: 444.
— [The women medical students at Zurich.] Boston medical and surgical journal, 89: 343. 1873.   *5746.1.89
— Zurich and female medical students. Boston medical and surgical journal, 88: 147. 1873.   *5746.1.88
Channing, Walter. Remarks on the employment of females as practitioners in midwifery. By a physician. Boston, 1820.
No. 21 in *5793.70
Chesney, Jesse Portman. Woman as a physician. Newmarket, Mo. [1871?]
From the Richmond and Louisville medical journal, 11: 1. 1871 [*7752.5.11].
Clark, A. R., and others. Revised case for pursuers in causa Sophia Louisa Jex-Blake and others against the Senatus academicus of the University of Edinburgh and chancellor thereof. [Edinburgh, 1873.]
Clarke, Edward Hammond. Medical education of women. Boston medical and surgical journal, 81: 345. 1869.   *5746.1.81
Cleaves, Margaret Abbie. The medical and moral care of female patients in hospitals for the insane. N. p. [1879.]   7805.63
— Memorial of Delia S. Irish, M.D., of Davenport. Transactions of the Iowa state medical society, 4: 187. 1880.   *7790.50 (1880)

Cleveland, Emeline Horton. Introductory lecture on behalf of the faculty to the class of the Female medical college of Pennsylvania. Phila., 1858.   No. 11 in *5793.70
— Valedictory address to the graduating class of the Female medical college of Pennsylvania, with announcement of the fourteenth annual session. Phila., 1863.
No. 13 in *5793.70
— Valedictory address to the graduating class of the Woman's medical college of Pennsylvania. Phila., 1868.   No. 14 in *5793.70
— Papers read at the memorial hour commemorative of Emeline H. Cleveland. [Phila., 1879.]   No. 10 in *4240a.53
Coates, Reynell. Introductory lecture to the class of the Female medical college of Pennsylvania. Phila., 1861.
Conditions of Miss Garrett's gift to the medical school of Johns Hopkins university. Boston medical and surgical journal, 128: 71. 1893.   *5746.1.128
Cordell, Eugene F. Woman as a physician. Baltimore, 1883.
Reprinted from Maryland medical journal, 10: 353. 1883–84 [*7792.60.10].
Cornell, William Mason. An introductory lecture to the class of the Female medical college of Pennsylvania. Phila., 1852.
No. 10 in *5793.70
Coues, Elliott. "A woman in the case." An address at the annual commencement of the National medical college, Washington, 1887. 2d ed., with an introduction by Elisabeth Cavazza. Boston, 1890. [Biogen series.]
3579.108
Cyon, E. de. École médicale pour les femmes à Saint-Pétersbourg. Paris, 1880.
Davies, Emily. Medicine as a profession for women. A paper read at the Social science congress. London, 1862.
Davis, Paulina Wright. Female physicians. Boston medical and surgical journal, 41: 520. 1850.   *5746.1.41
Dohrn, R. Ueber die Zulassung weiblicher Aerzte, speziell zur Ausübung der Geburtshülfe. Deutsche medicinische Wochenschrift, 19: 179. 1893.
Dolley, Sarah R. A. Closing lecture at the Woman's medical college of Pennsylvania. [Phila., 1874.]
Drysdale, Charles Robert.. Medicine as a profession for women. London, 1870.
Earle, Charles Warrington. The demand for a woman's medical college in the West. Waukegan, Ill., 1879.
Edinburgh. Executive committee for securing a complete medical education to women in Edinburgh. Medical education of women. Statement of accounts by the executive committee. Edinburgh, 1874.
Edinburgh school of medicine for women. Prospectus. Edinburgh, 1895.
— Report, 4th, 1892–94. Edinburgh, 1894.
Edmunds, James. The inaugural address delivered for the Female medical society. London. [1864.]
Erhard, Anna. Women physicians in Germany. [By A. vom Strande, pseud.] Trans. from "Frauenberuf." Chautauquan, 11: 625. 1890.

Fawcett, Millicent Garrett. The medical and general education of women. Fortnightly review, 10: 554. 1868. P R

Female medical education society. Annual report, 1st-6th. 1848-55. Boston, 1850-55. *7725.1

Later reports will be found under New England female medical college.

— Female medical education society and New England female medical college. Circular. Boston, 1853. 7726.7

— Report to the Massachusetts legislature, by the committee on education, in favor of an appropriation of $5,000 to the Female medical education society, with information respecting the society and the Boston female medical school. Boston, 1851.
No. 2 in *5793.70

Females as physicians. Boston medical and surgical journal, 53: 292. 1855. *5746.1.53

Fullerton, Anna M. Women students at Vienna. Philadelphia medical times, 15: 35. 1884-85. *5711.50.15

Fussell, Edwin. Valedictory address to the graduating class of the Female medical college of Pennsylvania. Phila., 1857.
No. 10 in *5712.53.1

— Valedictory address to the graduating class of the Female medical college of Pennsylvania. Phila., 1861. No. 12 in *5793.70

Garcia, M. A. Female physicians — the first one in America [Elizabeth Blackwell]. Detroit lancet, 2: 284. 1879.

Gassett, Helen Maria. Categorical account of the Female medical college, to the people of the New England states. Boston, 1855.
7739.100

General medical council, Great Britain. Debate on the admission of women to the profession. London. [1875.]

— Special education for women. Resolutions and report. London. [1873.]

Gertsenstein, G. M. Jenskie vrachebnie kursi. Statisticheskie materijali k istorii ich. [Medical lectures for women: statistics of attendance.] Vrach, 1: 553. 1880.

Girault, Augustine. La femme médecin, sa raison d'être au point de vue du droit, de la morale et de l'humanité. Par Mme A. Gael [pseud.]. Paris, 1868.

Glenn, Mrs. G. Are women as capable of becoming physicians as men? Clinic, 9: 243. 1875.

Great Britain. General council of medical education and registration. Special education of women. Resolutions and report on the education of women in midwifery, management of medical institutions, dispensing medicine and nursing. London. [1873.]

Gregory, George. Medical morals: designed to show the pernicious social and moral influence of the present system of medical practice, and the importance of establishing female medical colleges. N. Y., 1852.
No. 6 in *5790.3

Gregory, Samuel. Doctor or doctress? Boston, 1868. 7726.11

— Female physicians. From the Englishwoman's journal. [Boston, 1862.] 7726.12
Reprinted in Littell's living age, 3d series, 17: 243.

— Letter to ladies in favor of female physicians. Boston, 1850. 5773.17

— Same. 2d ed. 1854. No. 4 in *5793.70

— Same. 3d ed. 1856. 7777.28

— The war against the New England female medical college. Circular to the members of the Massachusetts legislature. Boston, 1866. 7726.8

Hartshorne, Henry. Valedictory address to the twentieth graduating class of the Woman's medical college of Pennsylvania. Phila., 1872. No. 13 in *5712.53.1

Harvard college. Medical school. The admission of women to Harvard university [medical school]. Boston medical and surgical journal, 100: 789. 1879. *5746.1.100

— Discussion in the board of overseers and the medical faculty on the admission of women to the Medical school [in consideration of the offer of $10,000 for that purpose by Miss Marian Hovey]. (Annual report of the president, 1878-79, pp. 29-32.)
*4493.1.(1878-79)

— Medical education of women. [Votes of the corporation and overseers, and protest of the medical faculty, upon the reception of a letter from Marie E. Zakrzewska, M.D., and nine others, offering $50,000 for the purpose of providing medical education for women.] (Annual report of the president, 1881-82, pp.32-38, 133-134.)
*4493.1 (1881-82)

— The medical education of women at Harvard; report of a committee of the overseers, Theodore Lyman, chairman. Medical news, 40: 476. 1882. *7715.1.40

— [Report of the committee to whom was referred the proposal of Miss Marian Hovey to give $10,000 to the Harvard medical school if its advantages could be offered to women on equal terms with men. Boston, 1878.] 7738.65

Harvard medical school, The, and women. Boston medical and surgical journal, 100: 727. 1879. *5746.1.100

Harvard university and female physicians. Boston medical and surgical journal, 102: 88. 1880. *5746.1.102

Henius, ——. Ueber die Zulassung der Frauen zum Studium der Medicin. Deutsche medicinische Wochenschrift, 21: 613. 1895.
*3720a.101.21

Hermann, Ludimar. Das Frauenstudium und die Interessen der Hochschule Zürich. Zürich, 1872.
From the Neue Züricher-Zeitung. Written in answer to Professor von Bischoff's "Studium u. die Ausübung der Medizin durch Frauen."

— and Katharina Gundling. Noch einmal das Frauenstudium. Beilage zur Allgemeinen Zeitung. 1872 (4): 4727. 6300.2.1872 (4)

Hoggan, Frances Elizabeth. Medical women for India. Contemporary review, 42: 267. 1882. P R

— Women in medicine [in Great Britain]. (Stanton, Theodore, editor. The woman question in Europe, pp. 63-89. 1884.)
3572.53

Hosmer, William. Appeal to husbands and wives in favor of female physicians. N. Y., 1853.

Humpal-Zeman, Josephine. Women physicians in Austria. Woman's journal, 24: 232. 1893. *7260.51.24

India. Surgeon-general. Lady medical students, Madras. Extracts from correspondence [on the subject of their admission to the Madras medical college]. Madras. [1875.]

Isambert, Émile. Du rôle médical des femmes. Paris, 1871.

Jacobi, Mary Putnam. Inaugural address at the opening of the Woman's medical college of the New York infirmary, Oct. 1, 1880 [on medical education]. Chicago medical journal and examiner, 42: 561. 1881.

— Shall women practice medicine? North American review, 134: 52. 1882.

— Woman in medicine. (Meyer, Annie N., editor. Woman's work in America, pp. 139–205. 1891.)   3575.119

Judson, Eliza Edmundson. Address in memory of Ann Preston, M.D. [Phila., 1873.]
                              No. 13 in *4441.69

K., A. C. Women at Johns Hopkins. Nation, 52: 71. 1891.   P R

King, Elizabeth T. The admission of women to the medical school of the Johns Hopkins university. (Transactions of the National council of women, 1891, pp. 199–203.) 5583.13

Lancaster, Henry Hill. Case for the Senatus academicus of the University of Edinburgh in declarator, etc. Miss S. L. Jex-Blake and others, pursuers; against them and the chancellor of said university, defenders. Reclaiming note boxed 29th August, 1872. [Edinburgh, 1873.]

— Appendix to case. [Edinburgh, 1873.] Appendix contains the charters of the universities of St. Andrews, Glasgow and King's college, Aberdeen; excerpts from "Repertorio di professori della celebre Università di Bologna"; letters from various German university professors, and from Prof. Donders of Utrecht.

Latimer, Caroline W. The medical profession. (Ladies at work, pp. 75–85. 1893.) 3574.112

London school of medicine for women. Prospectus. Session 1895/96. London, 1895.

— Report. 1877/78–1895/96. London, 1878–96.

Longshore, Joseph S. An introductory lecture at the opening of the Female medical college of Pennsylvania. Phila., 1850.
                              No. 7 in *5771.56

— Introductory lecture delivered in the female department of the Penn medical university, Oct. 1, 1860. Being a review of the action of the Pennsylvania state medical society in relation to female physicians and female medical colleges. Phila., 1861.

— The practical importance of female medical education; an introductory lecture delivered in the Pennsylvania medical college of Philadelphia. Phila., 1853.

— A valedictory address delivered before the graduating class at the first annual commencement of the Female medical college of Pennsylvania, Dec. 30, 1851. Phila., 1852.
                              No. 19 in *5712.53.1

—Valedictory address to the graduating classes of Penn medical university. Phila., 1857.

McCowen, Jennie. Women physicians in hospitals for the insane. (Papers read before the Association for the advancement of women, 1886, pp. 87–93.) *7572.70 (1886)

Manouvrier, L. L'internat (en médecine) des femmes. Revue scientifique, 34: 592. 1884.
                              *5292.1.34
Also in Tribune médicale, 16: 589, 601. 1884.

Markby, Thomas. Medical women. London, 1869.

Marshall, Mary A. Medicine as a profession for women. Woman's world, 1: 105. 1888.

Massachusetts. General court. Report by the committee on education in favor of an appropriation of $5,000 to the Female medical education society, with information respecting the society, and the Boston female medical school. Boston, 1851. No. 2 in *5793.70

— Report [of the committee on the judiciary, upon the petition of E. C. Rolfe and others in regard to the New England female medical college]. [Boston, 1866.] No. 8 in *5793.70

— [Report of the joint committee on education on petition praying for a grant of $10,000 in aid of the Female medical college. April 14, 1852.]

— [Report of the committee on education on the petition of the directors of the Female medical education society for a limited annual grant. April 27, 1854.]

Medical act, The, of 1858 in relation to the practice of medicine by women. [Edinburgh? 1873.]

Medical education of women. Edinburgh university magazine, March, 1871.

Medical society of the state of Pennsylvania. A brief history of proceedings, 1859–1871, to procure the recognition of women physicians by the medical profession of the state. Added, an account of the measures adopted, 1877–79, to procure a law to authorize trustees of hospitals for the insane poor, under control of the state, to appoint women physicians to have entire medical control of the insane of their sex. Phila., 1888.   5735.63

Medical women. Lancet, 110: 397. 1876.
                              *5743.1.110
Reprinted in the Victoria magazine, 27: 59.

Medical women. Victoria magazine, 31: 222. 1878.   P R

Medical women; or, qualified female medical practitioners. Leisure hour, 19: 709. 1870.
                              P R

Monroe, Harriet Earhart. Need of women physicians in Germany. Woman's tribune, April 23, 1892.   *N.1045.3 (1892)

Mueller, Peter. Ueber die Zulassung der Frauen zum Studium der Medizin. Hamburg, 1894. [Sammlung gemeinv. wissenschaftl. Vorträge.]   *5924.60.N.F.9

N., D. Coeducation at Johns Hopkins. Nation, 63: 175. 1896.   P R
There are brief articles on the same subject on pp. 159, 194, 230 of the same volume.

Neumann, Julius. Sollen Frauen zum Studium der Medicin zugelassen werden? Wiener klinische Wochenschrift, 7: 238. 1894.

New England female medical college. Annual advertisement, 6th. Boston, 1853. 7726.9

— Circular to the members of the House of representatives [in regard to incorporating the college]. [Boston, 1853.]
                              No. 1 in *7578.8

— Circular to the members of the Massachusetts legislature. [Dated, April 26, 1866.] Boston, 1866.   No. 4 in *7578.8

— Clinical department. Annual report. Boston, 1860.   *7779.31

— Copy of a petition [etc.] presented to the City government. [Boston, 1863, 64.]
No. 24 in *5720a.9
— Laying of the corner-stone, historical statement [etc.]. [Boston, 1870.] 7726.13
— Memorial to the Massachusetts legislature. Presented and received, May 17, 1866. Being a reply to the report of the judiciary committee of the House. Boston, 1866.
No. 5 in *7578.8
— Memorial to the Massachusetts legislature. Presented and received, May 21, 1866. [Boston, 1866.] No. 2 in *7578.8
— Statement to its patrons and friends. [Boston, 1866.] 7726.10
Northwestern university woman's medical school. Chicago clinical review, 3: 57. 1893-4.
Orvonök képzése. [The education of women-physicians.] Orvosi hetilap, 39: 301. 1895.
Pechey, Edith. Inaugural address delivered at the London school of medicine for women. London, 1878.
Penny, Mrs. Frank. Women's medical work in India. (Ladies at work, pp. 86–93. 1893.)
3574.112
"Philadelphia," pseud. Men and women medical students, and the woman movement. No. [1], 2. [Phila.] 1869, 70.
A protest against clinics before classes of both sexes.
Philadelphia county medical society. Women as physicians. Preamble and resolution upon the status of women as physicians, with a reply by a woman [Ann Preston]. [Phila., 1867.] No. 6 in *5793.70
Pope, Emily F., and others. The practice of medicine by women in the United States. [By] Emily F. Pope, Emma L. Call, C. Augusta Pope. [Boston, 1881.]
No. 8 in *5771.56
Reprinted from the Journal of social science, 14: 178.
Pozzi, Samuel Jean. Contre l'internat des femmes. Revue scientifique, 34: 536. 1884.
*5292.1.34
Also in Gazette médicale de Paris, 7e s., 1: 505. 1884 [*7772.1, sér. 7.1].
Practice of medicine by women in 1572. Medical record, 46: 562. 1894. *7741.1.46
Preston, Ann. Introductory lecture in the Female medical college of Pennsylvania for the session of 1855-56. Phila., 1855.
No. 4 in *5712.53.2
— Introductory lecture to the class of the Female medical college of Pennsylvania, at the opening of the tenth annual session. Phila., 1859.
— Valedictory address to the graduating class of the Female medical college of Pennsylvania for the session of 1857-58. Phila., 1858. No. 8 in *5712.53.2
— Valedictory address to the graduating class of the Female medical college of Pennsylvania, March 16, 1864, with announcement of the fifteenth annual session. Phila., 1864.
No. 11 in *5712.53.2
— Valedictory address to the graduating class of the Women's medical college of Pennsylvania, at the eighteenth annual commencement. Phila., 1870. No. 14 in *5712.53.2
Progress of the medical education of women in Europe. Medical and surgical reporter, 45: 550. 1881.

Putnam, James Jackson. Women at Zurich. Boston medical and surgical journal, 101: 567. 1879. *5746.1.101
Queen Margaret college, Glasgow. School of medicine for women. Prospectus, 1895-96. Glasgow, 1895.
Reeve, John Charles. The entrance of women into medicine. Cleveland, 1895. 7722.57
From the Western Reserve medical journal, 3: 345. 1894-5.
Richelot, Gustave. La femme-médecin. Paris, 1875.
Rose, Edmund. The experiment at Zurich. Professor Rose and Zurich female students. Boston medical and surgical journal, 101: 455. 1879. *5746.1.101
Roubinovitch, J. Une école de médecine pour femmes à Saint-Pétersbourg. Progrès médical, 3e sér., 1: 361. 1895.
Runge, Ferdinand. Die Krankenpflege als Feld weiblicher Erwerbsthätigkeit gegenüber den religiösen Genossenschaften. Im Anhange zu den Verhandlungen der Berliner Frauen-Vereins-Conferenz dargestellt. Berlin, 1870.
S***v***s. Die Frage der Zulassung der Frauen zum akademischen Studium vor den beiden Landes-Universitäten in Ungarn. Wiener medizinische Blätter, 3: 489. 1880.
Schacher, Polycarp Friedrich, and Johann Heinrich Schmid. Dissertatio historico-critica de feminis ex arte medica claris. Von Weibern die sich in der Arztneywissenschaft berühmt gemacht. Lipsiæ, 1738.
Schultze, Caroline. La femme-médecin au XIXe siècle. Paris, 1888.
Schwerin, Ludwig. Die Zulassung der Frauen zur Ausübung des ärztlichen Berufes. Berlin, 1880. [Deutsche Zeit- und Streit-Fragen.] No. 3 in *5216.50.9
Scottish association for the medical education of women and the Medical college for women. Annual report, 6th. N. p. 1896.
Scottish universities commission. Graduation and instruction of women in medicine. Lancet, 1892 (1): 661. *5743.1.1892 (1)
Simon, J., and G. Simon. La femme docteur et la femme pharmacien. Gazette médicale de Liége, 1891-2, 4: 361.
Späth, Joseph. Das Studium der Medizin und die Frauen. Rektorsrede. [Wien, 1872.]
Separat-Abdruck aus der Wiener medizinischen Presse, 13: 1109 [*7720.5.13].
Stansfeld, James. Medical women: an historical sketch. Edinburgh, 1878.
Reprinted, by the Edinburgh executive committee for securing a complete medical education to women, from the Nineteenth century, 1: 888. 1877.
Stellung, Die, der Edinburger Universität zur Frage des medicinischen Studiums der Frauen. Beilage zur Allgemeinen Zeitung, 1872 (4): 4222. *6300.2.1872 (4)
Stevenson, Sarah Hackett. Woman in medicine. (Report of the International council of women, 1888, pp. 169–173.) 5586.65
Reprinted from the Woman's tribune, March 30, 1888 [N.1045.3].
Tait, Lawson. The medical education of women. Birmingham medical review, 3: 81. 1874.
Thomas, Charles Hermon. Valedictory address [at the 21st annual commencement of the Woman's medical college]. 7738.74
Cut from the Philadelphia evening bulletin, March 12, 1873.

Tkatchef, Alexandrine. Les cours de méde-cine pour les femmes à St.-Pétersbourg. Gazette hebdomadaire des sciences médi-cales de Montpellier, 9: 301. 1887.

Trélat, Ulysse. L'internat des femmes. Ga-zette médicale de Paris, 7e s., 1: 529. 1884. *7772.1, sér. 7, 1

University of Edinburgh.. University law-suit. A brief summary of the action of declarator brought by ten matriculated lady students against the Senatus. Edinburgh. [1872?]

University of Michigan. Annual announce-ment of the department of medicine and sur-gery. 1870/71–96/97. Ann Arbor, 1870–96.

Velden, Friedrich von den. Die Ausübung der Heilkunde durch die Frauen, geschicht-lich betrachtet. Tübingen, 1892.

Waldeyer, W. Das Studium der Medizin und die Frauen. Wiener medizinische Blätter, 11: 1252. 1888.

Weilshaeuser, Emil. Weibliche Aerzte für Frauen, Mädchen und Kinder. Ein Wort zur Beherzigung für alle wahren Freunde des socialen Fortschritts. Berlin, 1868.

West, Charles. Medical women: a statement and an argument. London, 1878.

White, Frances E. The American medical woman. Medical news, 67: 123. 1895. *7715.1.67
Also in the Woman's medical journal, 4: 239. To-ledo, 1895.

Williams, Henry Willard. Female physicians. [Boston, 1856.] No. 5 in *5793.70
Reprinted from the Boston medical and surgical journal, 54: 3 [*5746.1.54].

Williams, N. A dissertation on female phy-sicians. Boston medical and surgical jour-nal, 43: 69. 1850. *5746.1.43

Wilson, John Stainback. Female medical edu-cation. Southern medical and surgical journal, n. s., 10: 1. 1854.

Wilson, Robert. Æsculapia victrix. Fort-nightly review, 45: 18. 1886.   P R

Woman's medical college, Chicago. Annual announcement, 1870–82. *7736.53

Woman's medical college of Pennsylvania. Catalogue and annual announcement. 1850/51–96/97. Phila., 1850–96.
— Constitution and report of the annual meet-ing of the Alumnæ association. Phila., 1878.

Woman's medical college of the New York infirmary. Annual catalogue and announce-ment. N. Y., 1869–96. 7738.72
— Report of the anniversary meeting of the Alumnæ association of the college. N.Y., 1871.

Women and medicine. Saturday review, 34: 641. 1872.   P R
A review of Sophia Jex Blake's Medical women.

Women as doctors. Every Saturday, 11: 27. 1871.   P R

Women physicians. Every Saturday, 6: 407. 1868.   P R

Women physicians. Macmillan's magazine, 18: 369. 1868.   P R

Women who practised medicine in ancient times. North American medical and chir-urgical review, 5: 372, 560. 1861.

X . . ., Mme. Pourquoi les femmes font de la médecine. Gazette hebdomadaire des sci-ences médicales de Montpellier, 7: 25. 1885.

Zakrzewska, Marie Elizabeth. Fifty years ago: a retrospect. Woman's medical jour-nal, 1: 193. Toledo, 1893.
On the position of women physicians fifty years ago.
— Introductory lecture, Nov. 2, before the New England medical college at the open-ing of the term of 1859–60. Boston, 1859. No. 8 in *5793.70

Zehender, Carl Wilhelm von. Ueber den Be-ruf der Frauen zum Studium und zur prak-tischen Ausübung der Heilwissenschaft. Vortrag gehalten am 15. Februar 1875 in der Aula der Universität Rostock. Rostock, 1875.

The Ministry.

Bartlett, Caroline J. Woman's call to the ministry. (World's congress of representa-tive women, pp. 229–235. 1894.) 5583.14

Boston university. School of theology. An-nual report, 1871/72, 72/73. Boston, 1872, 73. *4492.136
The report for 1871/72 contains a sketch of the origin and history of the institution.
— Catalogue, 1896/97, and circular 1897/98. Boston, 1897.
— Historical sketch. Note by R. S. Foster. Courses of instruction [etc.]. Boston, 1896.
This took the place of the catalogue for 1895/96.
— Official circular. Regulations relative to the degree of Doctor in sacred theology. [Boston, 1890?]
— Official circular. Subjects and treatises recommended to candidates for the degree of Doctor of sacred theology. [Boston, 1891.]
— Quadrennial report, 1876–80. [Boston, 1881.] *4492.137

Bowles, Ada C. Woman in the ministry. (Report of the International council of women, 1888, pp. 180, 181.) 5586.65
Reprinted from the Woman's tribune, March 30, 1888 [N.1045.3].
— Same (Meyer, Annie N., editor. Woman's work in America, pp. 206–217. 1891.) 3575.119

Cobbe, Frances Power. The fitness of women for the ministry. Theological review, 13: 239. 1876.   P R
— Same. (The peak in Darien, pp. 197–262. 1882.) 5444.72

Fitch, H. P. At the temple gate; or, the right of Christian women to the ministry. Hast-ings, Neb., 1890.

Frame, Nathan T. Shall women preach? Chicago, 1890.

Hanaford, Phebe Ann. Statistics of the wom-an ministry. (Papers read at the Congress of women, 1875, pp. 36–41.) *7572.70 (1875)
— Services at the ordination and installation of Phebe A. Hanaford, as pastor of the First universalist church in Hingham. Bos-ton, 1870. 3440a.83

Kollock, Florence E. Woman in the pulpit. (World's congress of representative women, pp. 221–228. 1894.) 5583.14

Safford, Mary A. Woman as a minister of religion. (World's congress of representa-tive women, pp. 236–241. 1894.) 5583.14

Sunderland, Jabez Thomas. The liberal Chris-tian ministry [as a calling for young men and young women]. Boston, 1889.

Tupper, Mila Frances. Present status of women in the church. (Transactions of the National council of women, 1891, pp. 98-107.)   *5583.13

Willard, Frances Elizabeth. Woman in the pulpit. Boston. [1888.]   5584.50

Woods, Kate Tannatt. Women in the pulpit. (Transactions of the National council of women, 1891, pp. 286-293.)   *5583.13

Science.

Becker, Lydia Ernestine. On the study of science by women. Contemporary review, 10: 386. 1869.   P R

Bolton, Sarah Knowles. Maria Mitchell. (Lives of girls who became famous, pp. 87-103. 1886.)   1538.29

Brackett, Anna Callender. Maria Mitchell. Century, 38: 954. 1889.   P R

Edwards, Matilda Barbara Betham. Caroline Herschel. (Six life studies of famous women, pp. 87-128. 1880.)   2247.62

Everett, Edward, editor. Correspondence relative to the award of the King of Denmark's comet medal to Miss Maria Mitchell. Cambridge, 1849.   5922.19

Herschel, Caroline Lucretia. Memoir and correspondence. By Mrs. John Herschel. London, 1876.   2547.61
— Same. N. Y., 1876.   2547.64

Jacobi, Mary Putnam. Woman in science. (With discussion.) (World's congress of representative women, 1894, pp. 195-208.)   5583.14

Lagrange, E. Women in astronomy. Popular science monthly, 28: 534. 1886.   P R
Translated from Ciel et terre.

Lewis, Grace Anna. Science for women. (Papers read at the Congress of women, 1875, pp. 63-73.)   7572.70 (1875)

Miller, Florence Fenwick. Only a satellite. Caroline Herschel. (In ladies' company, pp. 153-166. 1892.)   2259a.60

Mitchell, Maria. Life, letters, and journals. Compiled by Phebe Mitchell Kendall. Boston, 1896.   2345.104
Reviewed in the Independent, 49: 185. 1897 [*N.713.1.49].
— The need of women in science. (Papers read at the Congress of women, 1877, pp. 9-11.)
Reprinted in Victoria magazine, 28: 187.
— Reminiscences of the Herschels. Century, 38: 903. 1889.   P R

Newbury, Spencer Baird. New laboratory for physics and chemistry at Cornell university. Science, 1: 538. 1883.   P R

Patterson, John Stahl. Women and science. Radical, 7: 169, 287. 1870.   *7302.2.7

Reumont, Alfred von. Mary Somerville. (Historisches Taschenbuch. Jahrg. 47, pp. 179-248. 1877.)   *2309.1.47

Scientific education of women. Nature, 2: 117, 165. 1870.   P R

Sketch of Maria Mitchell. Appleton's Popular science monthly, 50: 544. 1897.   P R

Somerville, Mary. Personal recollections. With selections from her correspondence. By Martha Somerville. London, 1873.   2448.68
— Same. Boston, 1874.   2448.69

Spofford, Harriet Prescott. Maria Mitchell. Chautauquan, 10: 181. 1889.   P R

Stuart, James. The teaching of science [to women]. (Butler, Josephine E., editor. Woman's work and woman's culture, pp. 121-151. 1869.)   5573.34

Underwood, Sara A. Women's work in science. New England magazine, 9: 695. 1890-91.   P R

Walford, Lucy Bethiah. Mary Somerville. (Four biographies from "Blackwood," pp. 229-312. 1888.)   4547.113

Whitney, Mary Watson. In memoriam. Maria Mitchell. [1889.]
Printed, by special contribution, in behalf of the Maria Mitchell endowment fund.
— Life and work of Maria Mitchell, LL.D. (Papers read before the Association for the advancement of women, 1891, pp. 12-28.)   *7572.70 (1891)
— Scientific study and work for women. Education, 3: 58. 1882.   P R

V. Opportunities for Post-Graduate Study.

American school of classical studies at Athens. Annual report, 1st-4th, of the managing committee. 1881-1894/95. Cambridge. [1882?-] 96.   *2963.51

Association of collegiate alumnæ. Graduate study. [1883.]
— The European and American fellowship. [Circular regarding conditions, etc., for 1897/98.]
— Report of committee on endowment of fellowship. [1888?]

American woman, An, at the German universities. Nation, 64: 223. 1897.   P R

Barus, Annie Howes. Opportunities for advanced study. [Boston, 1884.]
Reprinted by the Association of collegiate alumnæ from the Vassar miscellany of April, 1884.

Benneson, Cora Agnes. College fellowships for women. (Report of the International council of women, 1888, pp. 77-80.) *5586.65
Printed first in the Woman's tribune, March 28, 1888; also in the Woman's journal, June 30, 1888.

Bennett, C. W. Post-graduate degrees. (Proceedings of the convocation of the University of the state of New York, 1883, pp. 217-224.)   *6361.2 (1883)

Boyer, Leonard. University women. Nation, 58: 212. 1894.   P R

Channing, Eva. A girl graduate at Leipzig. Atlantic monthly, 44: 788. 1879.   P R

Dwight, Timothy. Education for women at Yale. Forum, 13: 451. 1892.   P R

F., G. T. Pioneer women students in Germany. Nation, 64: 262. 1897.   P R

Franklin, Christine Ladd. The usefulness of fellowships. A paper presented to the Association of collegiate alumnæ. [Boston, 1880.]

Graduate courses. A handbook for graduate students. Announcements of advanced courses of instruction offered by ... colleges and universities of the United States, for 1893/94, 96/97. Boston, 1894, 96. 2 v.   3596.119

Graduate courses. Lists of advanced courses announced by twenty-one colleges or universities of the U. S. for 1895-96. C. A. Duniway, editor-in-chief. N. Y., 1895.
3596.125
Hadley, Arthur Twining. The admission of women as graduate students at Yale. Educational review, 3: 486. 1892.   P R
K., M. F. Women at the German universities. Nation, 58: 137. 1894.   P R
Luxenberg, Adele. Women at Leipzig. Nation, 59: 247. 1894.   P R
Maddison, Isabel, and others. Handbook of courses open to women in British, Continental and Canadian universities. Compiled for the Graduate club of Bryn Mawr college. N. Y., 1896.   3597.160
Reviewed under the heading "A guide for women studying in Europe" in the Critic, 27: 145. 1897. Also in the Nation, 63: 411.
Maltby, Margaret Eliza. A few points of comparison between German and American universities. An address before the Association of collegiate alumnæ, Oct. 31, 1896. N. p. [1897.]
Massachusetts institute of technology. Opportunities for college graduates. Boston, 1896.
Peck, Tracy. Notes on graduate instruction. Yale university. Abstract of an address. [Also, The university of Pennsylvania. Notes by Ida Wood. Boston? 1892.]
Steffens, J. B. Women at Leipzig university. Nation, 59: 268. 1894.   P R
— Women at the German universities. Nation, 58: 154. 1894.   P R
Student. Women at the German universities. Nation, 58: 193. 1894.   P R
Wheeler, B. I. A woman's doctorate at Heidelberg. Nation, 57: 483. 1893.   P R
Woman's education association. Foreign fellowships. [Circular regarding conditions, etc., for 1897-98.]
X. Women in the University [of Zürich]. Nation, 54: 72. 1892.   P R
Yale college. Graduate school. Courses of instruction, for 1896/97. New Haven, 1896.
*4495.27

VI.   Occupations and Opportunities for College-Bred Women.

Abbott, Frances M. College women and matrimony again. Century, 51: 796. 1896.   P R
— The pay of college women. North American review, 163: 337. 1896.   P R
Association of collegiate alumnæ. Compensation, in certain occupations, of women who have received college or other special training. Boston, 1896.
Reprinted from the 25th annual report of the Massachusetts Bureau of statistics of labor, 1895, pp. 1-47. Reviewed in the Outlook, 53: 503, under the title "Earnings of college women."
— Work for women in local history. [Boston, 1885.]
— The work of alumnæ associations. [Phila., 1889.]
Brief summary of the reports given at the quarterly meeting of the Association.
Avery, Mary L., and Clara French. The duty of the college graduate to the English language. Papers presented to the Association of collegiate alumnæ. [Boston, 1887.]
Backus, Helen Hiscock. The need and the opportunity of college-trained women in philanthropic work. A paper presented to the New York association of collegiate alumnæ. [N. Y., 1887.]
Baldwin, Catherine. Some results of the higher education of women. Century, 52: 958. 1896   P R
On the Women's university association for work in the poorer districts of London.
Bancroft, Jane M. Occupations and professions for college-bred women. Education, 5: 486. 1885.   P R
Barus, Annie Howes. The study of the development of children. A paper presented to the Association of collegiate alumnæ. [Boston, 1891.]
— What our college women are doing. Chatauquan, 11: 65. 1870.

Blackwell, Alice Stone, and others. Patriotism as an aim of collegiate training. Papers presented to the Association of collegiate alumnæ. [Ithaca, 1888.]
Brown, Helen Dawes. University extension. A paper presented to the Association of collegiate alumnæ. [Boston, 1889.]
Butler, George. Education considered as a profession for women. (Butler, Josephine E., editor. Woman's work and woman's culture, pp. 49-77. 1869.)   5573.34
Clark, Kate Upson. College girls and marriage. Leslie's illustrated weekly, 83: 39. 1896.   *6941.15.83
Congrès international de l'enseignement primaire. Paris, 1889. De la part qu'il convient de faire aux femmes dans l'enseignement primaire, comme institutrices, comme directrices d'établissement et comme inspectrices. Paris, 1889.
Crawford, Emily. Journalism as a profession for women. Contemporary review, 64: 362. 1893.   P R
Dewey, Melvil. Librarianship as a profession for college-bred women. An address delivered before the Association of collegiate alumnæ. Boston, 1886.   6194.42
Doughty, Frances Albert. College women in literature. Critic, 24: 209. 1896.   P R
Duffey, Eliza Bisbee. Women in literature. Victoria magazine, 28: 277. 1877.   P R
Earle, Martha B. Women librarians. Independent, 49: 230. 1897.   N.713.1.49
Faithfull, Emily. Woman's work with special reference to industrial employment. A paper read before the Society of arts. Victoria magazine, 17: 308. 1871.   P R
Fanton, Mary Annable. Architecture as a profession for women. Demorest's family magazine, 32: 454. 1896.

G., A. L. Women teachers at the university of Zürich. Nation, 53: 447, 466. 1891. P R

Gordon, Alice M. After-careers of university-educated women. Nineteenth century, 37: 955. 1895. P R
Reprinted in Littell's living age, 206: 110.

Hewins, Caroline Maria. Library work for women. Library journal, 16: 273. 1891. *6171.5.16

Hubert, Philip G., jr. Occupations for women. (The woman's book, pp. 1–76. 1894.) 4003.121

James, M. S. R. American women as librarians. The library, 5: 270. 1893. *2147.75.5
— Women librarians. The library, 4: 217. 1892. *2147.75.4

Kelley, Florence. The need of theoretical preparation for philanthropic work. A paper presented to the New York association of collegiate alumnæ. [N. Y., 1887.]

King, Alice. Woman's work. Argosy, 10: 350. 1870. P R

Knightley, Lady Louisa Mary. New employ-ments for educated women. New review, 9: 577. 1893. P R

Le Geyt, Alice B. The necessity of trades and professions for women. Victoria magazine, 25: 585. 1875. P R

Lewis, Frances W. The value of pedagogics to the college graduate. Presented to the Association of collegiate alumnæ. [Boston, 1888.]

Lord, Eleanor Louise. Educated women as factors in industrial competition. A paper presented to the Association of collegiate alumnæ. [Boston, 1891.]

Macdonald, Louisa. Educational work for women in Australia, chiefly New South Wales. (Proceedings of the International congress of education, Chicago, 1893, pp. 887–890.) *3592.145

Mackintosh, May. Women as professional teachers. Education, 7: 556. 1886–87. P R

Marriage of women college graduates. Nation, 50: 330. 1890. P R

Miller, Mary Mann. The college woman in literature. Critic, 24: 282. 1896. P R

Raymond, John Howard. The mission of educated women. A baccalaureate sermon. Hackensack, N. J., 1871.
Also appended to his Life and letters, pp. 725–738. 1881 [4340a.127].

Registration of women teachers. Blackwood's magazine, 161: 83. 1897. P R

Richards, Ellen Henrietta. The relation of college women to progress in domestic sci-ence. A paper presented to the Association of collegiate alumnæ. [Chicago, 1890.]

Richardson, Miss. Librarianship as a profes-sion for women. The library, 6: 137. 1894. *2147.75.6

Salomon, Mathilde. De la part des femmes dans la propagation des langues vivantes. Paris, 1894. 3596.143

Sangster, Margaret Elizabeth. Editorship as a profession for women. Forum, 20: 445. 1895. P R

Scudder, Vida Dutton. The effect on charac-ter of a college education [and] The edu-cated woman as a social factor. Christian union, April 7, 14, and 21, 1887. P R
— The relation of college women to social need. A paper presented to the Association of collegiate alumnæ. [Boston, 1890.]

Sewall, May Wright. The domestic and so-cial effects of the higher education of wom-en; read before the Western association of collegiate alumnæ. [Ann Arbor? 1888?]
— Women as educators. (Papers read before the Association for the advancement of women, 1887, pp. 118–129.) *7572.70 (1887)

Shinn, Milicent Washburn. The marriage of college-bred women. Overland monthly, 15: 443. 1890. P R
— Marriage rate of college women. Century, 50: 946. 1895. P R
— On the rate of marriages among college women. Overland monthly, 11: 442, 1888; 13: 556, 1889. P R

Soper, Grace Weld. The occupations of wom-en college graduates. Harper's bazar, 21: 2, 18. 1888. *5400.1.21

Starrett, Helen Ekin. The future of educated women. Chicago, 1885. 5576.37
— After college, what? — for girls. N. Y., 1896. 5576.102
— The future of our daughters. Forum, 10: 185. 1890. P R

Stone, Lucinda H. A demand for women in the faculties of co-educational colleges and uni-versities. (Transactions of the National council of women, 1891, pp. 169–178.) *5583.13

Thwing, Charles Franklin. What becomes of college women? North American review, 161: 546. 1895. P R

Woolson, Abba Goold. Woman's work in edu-cation. Granite monthly, 3: 11. 1879. P R

VII.   Colleges and Universities Wholly or Partly Open to Women.

Antioch. (1852.)

Articles of incorporation of Antioch college. [Yellow Springs?] 1859.
— Same. Xenia, 1875.

Catalogue, 1853/54–96/97. Yellow Springs, 1853–96.
No catalogue was published for 1864/65 or for 1881/82.

Dedication of Antioch college and inaugural address of its president, Horace Mann. Yel-low Springs, 1854. 4487.26
— Same. Dayton, 1884.

Laws and regulations. [Yellow Springs, 1883.] 4487.26

Memorial exercises for the centenary of the birth of Horace Mann, to be held in Antioch college, June 16, 1896. .[Yellow Springs, 1896.]

[Programme of the course of instruction, etc. Yellow Springs, 1853.] No. 6 in *4494.9
Antiochian. Vol. 1-22 (no. 8). Yellow Springs, 1874-97.
Allen, Ira W. History of Antioch college. [Yellow Springs. Before 1859.]
— Rejoinder to [his] "pseudo" History of Antioch college. Yellow Springs, 1859.
No. 5 in *4487.25
Antioch college. Old and new, 4: 510. 1871.
P R
Bellows, Henry Whitney. The claims of Antioch college on the Unitarian denomination, inferred from a brief history of the institution. [Anon.] Boston, 1865.
No. 4 in *7452.62
— and others. Appeal on behalf of Antioch college, with a statement of its financial history, condition and prospects. N. Y., 1858.
No. 1 in *4494.9
Charles, Thomas. Reminiscences of Horace Mann while at Antioch college. Kindergarten magazine, 8: 626. 1896. *7224.10.8
Dean, A. S. Antioch college. [Yellow Springs? 1853.] No. 5 in *4494.9
Historical sketch of Antioch college. N. p. [After 1873.]
Hosmer, F. L. Antioch college. Christian register, 74: 421. 1895. *N.250.1.74
Hosmer, James Kendall. The drama in colleges. [Boston, 1872.] 4498.107
This has special reference to dramatic work at Antioch, and was originally published under the title, "The new wrinkle at Sweetbrier," in the Atlantic monthly, 30: 19.
Jones, Jenkins Lloyd. Four commencements. New unity, 1 (n. s.): 258. 1895.
Long, D. A. Sketch of the legal history of Antioch college. Dayton, 1890.
Mann, Mary Tyler. Life of Horace Mann. Boston, 1865. 4348.21
— Same. 2d ed. 4348.3
See chapter 6, pp. 383 et seq., for an account of Mann's connection with Antioch college.
Weston, J. B. Antioch college. The library and the school, 1 (no. 5): 1. 1879.

Boston University. (1869.)

General catalogue, 1872/73. [Cambridge.] 1873. 4393.66
Historical register. 1869-91. Boston, 1891.
4383.102
President's annual report, 1st-[21st]. 1873/74-95/96. Boston. [1874]-97. *2384.15
The 15th report is entitled The twenty years of Boston university, 1869-89; the 18th, The origin and progress of Boston university.
Year book. Edited by the university council. Vol. 1-24. Boston, 1874-97. *4386.75
School of all sciences. Official circular. Revised regulations for the degree Master of arts and Doctor of philosophy. [Boston, 189-?]
— Subjects and treatises recommended to candidates for the degree of Master of arts and Doctor of philosophy. [Boston, 1890.]
Hub, The. Published [annually] by the Junior class of the College of liberal arts. Boston, 1885-96.
Index, The. A university directory. Vol. 1-11. 1886/87-96/97. [Boston, 1886-96.]

University Beacon, published semi-monthly during the college year, by the University Beacon association of the College of liberal arts. Vol. 1-22. Boston, 1876-97. *4500.28
The title has twice been changed, and the intervals of publication have varied.
University convocation. Epsilon chapter. The Epsilon. Addresses of the graduates of the College of liberal arts. No. 1, 2. [Boston.] 1896, 97.

Bryn Mawr. (1885.)

Addresses at the inauguration of Bryn Mawr college, 1885. Phila., 1887.
Handbook of courses open to women in British, Continental and Canadian universities. Compiled for the Graduate club of Bryn Mawr college, by Isabel Maddison [and others]. N. Y., 1896.
Reviewed in the Nation, 63: 411; also, under the title "A guide for women studying in Europe," in the Critic, 27: 145. 1897 [P R].
President's report to the Board of trustees, 1884/85-94/95. Phila., 1885-96.
The first two were not published.
Program, 1885/86-96/97. Phila., 1885-96.
Program of graduate courses, 1891/92-96/97. Phila., 1891-96.
Abbott, Madeline Vaughan. Bryn Mawr college. New cycle, 8: 894. 1895. *5583.16.8
— Bryn Mawr college. Frank Leslie's popular monthly, 43: 23. 1897.
B., H. B. Bryn Mawr college. Woman's journal, 18: 364. 1887. *7260.51.18
Benneson, Cora Agnes. Bryn Mawr. Woman's journal, 22: 54. 1891. *7260.51.22
Bryn Mawr college. The [Syracuse] Academy, 2: 154. 1887. P R
Gage, Kitty M. Bryn Mawr college for women. Education, 7: 25. 1886. P R
North, Helen Marshall. A day at Bryn Mawr college. Demorest's family magazine, 32: 644. 1896. *7271.1.32
Smith, Alys Whitall Pearsall. A woman's college in the United States [Bryn Mawr]. Nineteenth century, 23: 918. 1888. P R
Wheeler, Emily F. Bryn Mawr college for women. Independent, 1888: 740. *N.713.1

Columbia.

Barnard college. Degrees given by Columbia college, 1890-91. [N. Y., 1891.] 4481.58
Collegiate course for women. (Handbook of information, 1885/86-88/89.) 2389a.64
Collegiate education of women. Circular of information, 1883-88/89. [N. Y., 1883-89.]
4481.57
Barnard, Frederick Augustus Porter. The higher education of women. Passages from the annual reports of the president of Columbia college. 1879-81. N. Y., 1882.
Fulton, John. Memoirs of Frederick A. P. Barnard. N. Y., 1896. 2342.114
Pp. 407-423 record Pres. Barnard's efforts to open Columbia to women. See review in Educational review, 12: 293 [P R], and in the Bookman, 4: 475 [P R].
Godkin, Edwin Lawrence. The Columbia college scheme of female education. Nation, 36: 484. 1883. P R

Runkle, Lucia Gilbert. A new knock at an old door. Century, 25: 683. 1883.   P R
In behalf of the petition to admit women to Columbia.

Sedgwick, Arthur George. Educating women. Nation, 36: 118. 1883.   P R
In behalf of the petition to admit women to Columbia.

Barnard. (1889.)

Circular of information, 1889/90. [N. Y., 1889.]   *4494.286

Courses in history, economics and sociology, 1896–97. [N. Y., 1896.]   4494.284

Courses in the department of pure science, 1896–97. [N. Y., 1896.]   *4494.288

Courses in the School of arts leading to the degree of Bachelor of arts in Columbia college, 1895–96. [N. Y., 1895.]

Courses in the School of philosophy of Columbia university in philosophy, psychology and education, linguistics and literature, 1896–97. [N. Y., 1896.]   *4494.287

Dean's annual report. [1895/96.] N. Y., 1896.

Meeting of trustees and associate members, Nov., 1890, 91. [N. Y., 1890, 91.]   *4494.282

Plans of the new building in the Boulevard at 119th street. [N. Y., 1896?]   *4494.289

Reports of the Dean and Treasurer, 1894–95. N. Y., 1895.   4494.283

Treasurer's report, 1889–95/96. [N. Y., 1893–96.]

Barnard college. Outlook, 53: 734, 888. 1896.   P R

Barnard's good fortune. Critic, 25: 358. 1896.   P R

Croly, Jennie Cunningham. Barnard college. New cycle, 8: 927. 1895.   5583.16.8

[Dedication of its new buildings.] Outlook, 54: 759. 1896.   P R

Meyer, Annie Nathan. Barnard college. Harper's bazar, 29: 443. 1896.   *5400.1.29

— The new home for Barnard college. Harper's bazar, 29: 938. 1896.   *5400.1.29

— A new phase of woman's education in America: Barnard college. (Transactions of the National council of women, 1891, pp. 178–188.)   *5583.13

New college, A, for women. Century, 38: 949. 1889.   P R

Cornell. (1872.)

Annual report of the president, 1880/81–95/96. Ithaca, 1881–96.   *4385.102
The report for 1882 and those previous to 1881 were never published.

Catalogue of the graduates. Cambridge. [1883.]   *4487.101

Courses of instruction in the President White school of history and political science, 1894–95. Ithaca, 1894.   *4484.143

Laws and documents relating to Cornell university, 1862–83. Ithaca, 1883.

Proceedings and addresses at the 25th anniversary. Ithaca, 1893.   *4481.122

Proceedings at the laying of the corner stone of the Sage college of the Cornell university, May 15, 1873. Added, a report [by A. D. White] to the trustees on the establishment of said college. Ithaca, 1873.   4487.7

Register, 1873/74–96/97. Ithaca, 1873–96.   *7595.9

Sage college for women, Cornell university. Ithaca, 1884.

Scholarships, fellowships and other aid to meritorious students. Ithaca, 1884.

Students' handbook. Ithaca, 1885–.

Ten year book, 1868–88. Ithaca, 1878, 88. 2 v.   *2386.26

Tribute to Henry W. Sage from the women graduates of Cornell university. Ithaca, 1895.

University guide, containing an account of the buildings and collections of Cornell university. Ithaca, 1875.

Cornell era. Vol. 1–   Ithaca, 1868–.

Cornell daily sun. Vol. 1–   Ithaca, 1880–.

Cornell magazine. Vol. 1–   Ithaca, 1888–.

Badger, Henry Clay. The Cornell university. Unitarian review, 18: 313. 1882.   P R

Brackett, Anna Callender. Coeducation at Cornell. New England journal of education, 7: 137. 1878.   *7590.8.7
Reprinted in Victoria magazine, 31: 218.

Cornell, Alonzo Burton. Biography of Ezra Cornell, founder of the Cornell university. N. Y., 1884.   4247.59
Notice of Sage college, pp. 209–211.

Hewett, Waterman Thomas. The history of Cornell university, 1868–93. (Selkreg, J. H. Landmarks of Tompkins county. 1894.)

Perkins, Frank Clinton. Cornell university: her general and technical courses. N. Y., 1891.   *4484.108

White, Andrew Dickson. Report submitted to the trustees of Cornell university, in behalf of a majority of the committee on Mr. Sage's proposal to endow a college for women. Ithaca, 1872. No. 5 in 4386.65

— The Sage college at the Cornell university. [Ithaca, 1876.]   4498.124

— Sage college at the Cornell university; circular in reply to inquiries about the facilities for the education of young ladies at the Cornell university. [Ithaca.] 1879.

Harvard.

See also Radcliffe.

Examinations for women, 1874–94. Cambridge, 1873–93.   *4483.119

Papers used at the examinations for women, 1874–79. Cambridge, 1876–79.   *4483.185

Report of the committee appointed to act for the faculty upon the returns made from the examinations for women. (Annual report of the president, 1873–74, pp. 87–90.)   *4493.1 (1873–74)

— Second report of the committee. (Annual report of the president, 1877/78, pp. 150–157.)   *4493.1 (1877–78)
This report covers the whole period of five years since the holding of the first examinations.

— Third [and last] report of the committee. (Annual report of the president, 1879–80, pp. 145–149.)   *4493.1 (1879–80)

Specimen papers for the examinations for women, 1881. Cambridge, 1881.   4483.184

Dean, Ellen. The Harvard examinations for women. (Annual report of the Superintendent of public instruction of the state of Michigan for 1879, pp. 142–147.)   *7598..56 (1879)

Dunbar, Charles Franklin. Reply to Dr. Stillé's strictures on the Harvard examinations for women. [Phila.; 1878.] *4493.136
Reprinted from the Penn monthly, 9: 284 [P R].

Harvard examinations for women. Old and new, 8: 371. 1873.   P R

Norris, Mary Harriott. Harvard examinations for women. New England journal of education, 7: 154. 1878.   *7590.8.7

Pennsylvania university and the Harvard examinations for women. Nation, 26: 183. 1878.   P R
Correspondence. Communications from Mrs. Wister, Elizabeth C. Ralston and R. H. Chase.

Stillé, Charles Janeway. The higher education of women and the Harvard examinations. Penn monthly, 9: 93. 1878.   P R

Wister, Sarah Butler. Harvard examinations for women. Penn monthly, 8: 944. 1877.   P R

— Harvard examinations for women. Nation, 26: 133. 1878.   P R
In reply to T. W. Higginson, in the Woman's journal of Jan. 12, and C. J. Stillé in the Press of Jan. 30.

Woman's education association. Harvard examinations for women, 1875-79. [Boston, 1874-78.]   *4483.118

Women at Harvard. Literary world, 13: 396. 1882.   P R

McGill. (1884.)

Annual calendar, 1884/85-96/97. Montreal, 1884-96.   *4484.103

Annual report for 1894. Montreal, 1894.

Examination papers. Session of 1885/6, 86/7. Montreal, 1886, 87.   3599.103
Later papers are in the Calendar.

Graduates, corrected to Jan., 1895. Montreal, 1895.

Dawson, Sir John William. Thirty-eight years of McGill. Montreal, 1893. 4480a.103

Massachusetts Institute of Technology. (1865.)

Annual catalogue. 1865/66-96/97. Boston, 1865-96.   *7592.9

Annual report of the president and treasurer. 1889-96. Boston, 1890-97.   *4493.56

A brief account of its foundation, character, and equipment. Boston, 1893-95.

The course in general studies. Boston, 1888-96.

Opportunities for teachers. Boston, 1895.

President's report, 1872/73-88. Boston, 1873-89.   *4493.56

Nichols, William Ripley. Publications of the Institute and of its officers, students and alumni. 1862-81. Boston, 1882.   *6173.25
— Same. 2d ed.   *6173.31
— Same. 1862-87. 2d ed. Rev. by L. M. Norton. Boston, 1888.   *6173.29
The Institute also publishes circulars of the departments of Architecture, Physics, Chemistry, Biology, etc., of the Lowell school of design and of the summer courses.

Mount Holyoke. (1837, 1888, 1893.)

Annual, 1837-96/97. Amherst [etc.], 1837-97.   *2387.21

[Circular to] candidates for Mount Holyoke seminary. N. d.

Female education. Tendencies of the principles embraced and the system adopted in the Mount Holyoke female seminary. [South Hadley, 1839.]   4498.155

General catalogue of officers and students. 1837-87. With appendix, 1887-89. [Springfield.] 1889.   4390.63

General view of the principles and design of the Mount Holyoke female seminary. Published by direction of the trustees. Boston, 1837.   4390.70

Memorandum society.. Catalogue [quinquennial], for 1842-67, 77. Amherst [etc.], 1843-78. 3 v.   *4381.50
The catalogue for 1877 includes a catalogue of the alumnæ.

Memorial. Twenty-fifth anniversary of the seminary. South Hadley, 1862.   4397.40

Opening of Lyman Williston hall. Address by W. S. Tyler and exercises of dedication. Springfield, 1877.   4498.159

Preparation for admission. [Circular.] South Hadley, 1840.

Quinquennial catalogue of officers and students, 1837-95. [South Hadley, 1895.]   4498.68

Semi-centennial celebration, 1837-87. [Springfield.] 1888.
Edited by Mrs. Sarah D. Stow.

Bittinger, Joseph Baugher. An address [on the life and work of Mary Lyon] at the laying of the corner stone of the Lake Erie female seminary, Painesville, O. Cleveland, 1857.

Clark, Nathaniel George. Spirit and purpose of Mount Holyoke seminary and college. An address at the fifty-first anniversary. Springfield, 1888.
This includes the address of Prof. W. S. Tyler to the graduating class.

Cowles, John Phelps. Pioneers in the education of women: Miss Z. P. Grant (Mrs. Wm. B. Banister). Barnard's journal of education, 30: 611. 1880.   P R

Fisk, Fidelia. Recollections of Mary Lyon, with selections from her instructions. Boston. [1866.]   7559.34

Gould, Elizabeth Porter. Mary Lyon. Education, 5: 506. 1885.   P R

Guilford, Lucinda T., compiler. The use of a life: memorials of Mrs. Z. P. Grant Banister. N. Y. [1886.]   4245.55
Chapter 6 and part of chapter 10 were written by Mrs. E. C. Cowles, of Ipswich, the intimate friend and associate of both Miss Lyon and Miss Grant.

Historical sketch of Mount Holyoke seminary. Springfield, 1876.

Hitchcock, Edward. A chapter in the book of Providence: the twelfth anniversary address. Amherst, 1849.   4390.62
On the character and work of Mary Lyon.

— The power of Christian benevolence illustrated in the life and labors of Mary Lyon. Northampton, 1851.   2344.17
— Same. 6th ed. 1852.   4445.300
— Same. New ed., abridged and in some parts enlarged [by Mrs. E. C. Cowles]. N. Y. [1858.]

Hooker, Henrietta Edgecomb. Mount Holyoke college. New England magazine, 21: 545. 1896-97.   P R

Humphrey, Heman. The shining path. A sermon preached in South Hadley at the funeral of Mary Lyon. Northampton, 1849.
4444.181

Lyon, Mary. [Circular in behalf of Mount Holyoke seminary, probably issued in 1836.]
— [Information concerning the qualifications for admission into Mount Holyoke female seminary, signed M. L., and dated South Hadley, Sept., 1835.]

Mary Lyon. Education, 5: 506. 1885.   P R

Massachusetts. General court. [Report of the committee on education, recommending an appropriation of $40,000 to Mount Holyoke seminary.] [Boston.] 1868. [Senate doc. no. 136.]
4390.68

Memorial service held in honor of Miss Mary A. Brigham, Brooklyn, Nov. 6, 1889. Published by the N. Y. and Brooklyn association of Holyoke alumnæ. N. Y., 1890.

North, Helen Marshall. Mount Holyoke college. New cycle, 8: 900. 1895.   5583.16.8
— At Mt. Holyoke college. Demorest's family magazine, 32: 518. 1896.

Nutting, Mary O. Historical sketch of Mount Holyoke seminary; prepared in compliance with an invitation from the Commissioner of education. Springfield, 1876.   4495.172
— Same. Washington, 1876.   4495.275
— Same. Springfield, 1878.
— Mount Holyoke female seminary, South Hadley. American journal of education, 30: 589. 1880.   P R
Abridged from the preceding.
— Mount Holyoke seminary. (Brackett, Anna C. The education of American girls, pp. 318–328. 1874.)   3599.161

Past and present of Mount Holyoke college. Harper's weekly, 41: 186. 1897.   P R

Stow, Sarah D. The growth of Mount Holyoke seminary: a paper read at the annual meeting of the National association of Holyoke alumnæ. Springfield, 1889.
— History of Mount Holyoke seminary during its first half century, 1837–87. [Springfield.] 1887.   4390.64

Wright, G. Frederick. Mary Lyon and Oberlin. Nation, 63: 436. 1896..   P R

Northwestern. (1869.)

Catalogue, 1869/70–95/96. Evanston, 1869–95.

Financial report of the treasurer and business agent, made to the Board of trustees, 1869/70–95/96. Evanston, 1870–96.

Northwestern university record. Published under the authority of the University. Vol. 1-3. Evanston, 1894–96.

President's annual report. 1869/70–95/96. Evanston, 1870–96.

The Northwestern. Vol. 1-17. Evanston, 1881–97.

Syllabus. No. 1-12. Evanston, 1885–96.
Published annually by the students.

Oberlin. (1833.)

Catalogue. 1839/40–96/97. Oberlin, 1839–96.
4499.56

Descriptive and historical sketches. Statistics. Its building era illustrated and described. Akron, Ohio, 1887.   4498.113

[History, list of officers, etc.] Chicago, 1893.
4486.137

Laws and regulations. [From 1867. Revised and republished from time to time until the present.]

Quinquennial catalogue. Oberlin, 1895.
4497.19

Reports of the president and treasurer. [Oberlin, 1891.]   4496.297

Schedule of courses in the department of philosophy and the arts, 1896/7. [Oberlin, 1896.]   4496.330

Semi-centennial register of the officers and alumni. Chicago, 1883.   2382.59

Triennial catalogue. Oberlin [etc.]. 1851–89.
4497.14

Ballantine, William Gay, editor. The Oberlin jubilee, 1833-1883. Oberlin. [1883.]
4388.101
"Reunion of alumnæ." Addresses by Mrs. A. A. F. Johnston, Mrs. Sarah C. Little, Mrs. Douglass Putnam, Mrs. M. C. Kincaid, Miss Mary Evans, with poem by Mrs. Emily Huntington Miller, pp. 142-191; "Oberlin and woman," by Mrs. Lucy Stone, pp. 311-321.

Fairchild, Edward Henry. Historical sketch of Oberlin college. Springfield, 1868.
4497.280

Fairchild, James Harris. Coeducation at Oberlin. Bibliotheca sacra, 46: 443. 1889.   P R
— Coeducation of the sexes [at Oberlin]: an address before a meeting of college presidents at Springfield, Ill. American journal of education, 17: 385. 1868.   P R
Reprinted in the Annual report of the U. S. Bureau of education, 1868, pp. 385-400 [*7595.1.1868].
— Educational arrangements and college life at Oberlin. Inaugural address. N. Y., 1866.   4496.140
— Oberlin: its origin, progress, and results. An address, Aug. 22, 1860. Oberlin, 1860.
4489.40
— Same. With an appendix by J. M. Ellis. 1871.   4489.37
— Oberlin: the colony and the college. 1835-83. Oberlin, 1883.   4388.102

Johnston, Adelia Antoinette Field. Oberlin college. (Brackett, Anna C. The education of American girls, pp. 329-345. 1870.)
3599.161

Oberlin college. Harper's weekly, 31: 786. 1887.   P R

Shumway, Arthur Leon, and Charles De Witt Brower. Oberliniana. A jubilee volume of semi-historical anecdotes connected with the past and present of Oberlin college, 1833-83. Cleveland. [1883?]   4388.100

Smith, Delazon. A history of Oberlin; or, new lights of the West. Cleveland, 1837.
4388.103

Tuttle, Eugene Albert. Oberlin college. Our continent, 2: 737. 1882.   *5335.50.2

Wright, G. Frederick. Mary Lyon and Oberlin. Nation, 63: 436. 1896.   P R

Queen's College, London. (1853.)

Calendar, 1895/96, 96/97. London, 1895, 96.

Radcliffe. (1894.)

Previous to 1894, this had been known as the Society for the collegiate instruction of women, incorporated in 1882. Earlier circulars and reports bore the title "Private collegiate instruction for women."

Announcement of courses of instruction, 1894/95-96/97. [Cambridge, 1894-96.] 4485.170
Annual reports of the president and treasurer, 1895/96. Cambridge, 1896.
Circular no. 1-4 [giving requirements for admission and courses of study for 1879/80. Cambridge, 1879, 80].
Courses of study, with the requirements for admission, 1880/81-93/94. Cambridge, 1880-93.
Extracts from letters of pupils. [Cambridge.] 1883.
Radcliffe college. (Harvard university catalogue, 1896/97, pp. 555-559.)
*4388.20 (1896-97)
Report of the dean to the president of the university, 1894/95, 95/96. (Annual reports of the president and treasurer of Harvard college, 1894/95, pp. 250-252; 1895/96, pp. 254-256.) *4493.1
Report of the ladies of the executive committee. Letters from the professors and the pupils. Cambridge, 1884.
Report of the president, dean, regent and treasurer, 1894/95. Cambridge. 1895. 4485.187
Reports of the president, regent and treasurer, 1893/94. Cambridge, 1894.
Reports of the treasurer and secretary, 1881/82 -92/93. Cambridge, 1880-93.
Requirements for admission, 1894-97. Cambridge. [1894-97.]
Association of collegiate alumnæ. Report of committee on the proposed charter for Radcliffe college. 1894.
Baldwin, Catherine. The appeal of the Harvard annex: a claim on educated women. Century. 28: 791. 1884. P R
Brooks, Frona Marie. How one "Annex maid" began her career. Wide awake, 25: 107. 1887.
Gilman, Arthur. Fay house of Radcliffe college. Harvard graduates' magazine, 4: 555. 1896. *4380a.100.4
— Radcliffe college. (The Cambridge of eighteen hunred and ninety-six, pp. 174-186. 1896.) 2355.76
— The Society for the collegiate instruction of women, commonly called "the Harvard annex." The story of its beginnings and growth ... Cambridge, 1891. 4493.216
Reprinted, with additions and changes from the Cambridge tribune, June, 1890.
— Teachers in colleges for women. Nation, 52: 178. 1891. P R
Applies entirely to Radcliffe.
Greeley, Miriam Mason. Radcliffe college. New cycle, 8: 917. 1895. *5583.16.8
Harvard annex. Vassar miscellany, 11: 229. 1882.
The Harvard annex and the university. Nation, 56: 28. 1893. P R
Signed by Mrs. Louis Agassiz, Mrs. George H. Palmer, and Katharine P. Loring.
Harvard annex girls. Where and how they pursue their studies. Boston Herald, July 10, 1888.

Kinney, Mary Kendrick. Women's colleges: the Harvard annex. Harper's bazar, 21: 683. 1888. *5400.1.21
Rand, Edward Augustus. A visit to the Harvard annex. Education, 2: 415. 1883. P R
Reed, Helen Leah. Radcliffe college. Harper's bazar, 29: 871. 1896. *5400.1.29
Smith, Minna Caroline. The Harvard annex. Education, 6: 568. 1886. P R
Warner, Joseph Bangs. Radcliffe college. Cambridge, 1894.
Reprinted from the Harvard graduates' magazine, 2: 329 [*4380a.100.2].
See also articles contributed regularly to the Harvard graduates' magazine.

Royal University of Ireland. (1882.)

Report, 13th. 1894. Dublin, 1895. [Great Britain. Parliament. Sessional papers.]
F.-R. C. 1895, vol. 28

Alexandra.

Ferguson, Mary Catharine Guinness, Lady. Alexandra college, Dublin. Woman's world, 1: 129. 1888.

Queen's College, Belfast.

Report of the President, 1894-95. Dublin, 1895. [Great Britain. Parliament. Sessional papers.] F.-R. C. 1895, vol. 28

Queen's College, Galway.

Report of the President. Dublin, 1895. [Great Britain. Parliament. Sessional papers.]
F.-R. C. 1895, vol. 28

Smith. (1875.)

Addresses at the inauguration of Rev. L. Clark Seelye as president of Smith college, and at the dedication of its academic building. Springfield, 1875. 4495.254
Official circular, 1-23. Northampton, 1874-96. 4386.105
Pamphlet of information concerning courses of study, 1895/96, 96/97. [Northampton? 1895, 96.]
Smith monthly. Oct., 1893-May, 1897. [Northampton, 1894-97.]
Alumnæ association of Smith college. Register of the alumnæ. 1887/88-1896/97. [Westfield, 1887-96.]
Ayres, Winifred. Smith college. Godey's magazine, 131: 25. 1895.
Description of Smith college. [N. Y., 1877.] 4497.297
Reprinted from Scribner's monthly, 14: 9. 1877.
Elektra, The, at Smith college. Literary world, 20: 225. 1889. P R
Eliot, Charles William. President Eliot at Smith college. New England journal of education, 10: 149. 1879. P R
Girton college and Smith college. Nation, 22: 112. 1876. P R
A comparison: favorable to Smith.
Greene, John Morton. An address at the centennial of the birth of Sophia Smith. With notes appended, printed by the college. [Northampton? 1896.]
— Early history of Smith college. Hampshire gazette, July 31, 1891-April 12, 1893.
Twelve letters published at irregular intervals during these years.

— Smith college and its founder. Abridged from an address at the opening of the college, July 14, 1875. American journal of education, 27: 617. 1877. P R

Hilliard, Caroline Elizabeth. Smith college. An historical sketch. Education, 8: 12. 1887. P R

Hurd, Mabel. How college girls can produce a Shakespearean play. Illustrated American, 21: 41. 1896. P R

Johnson, Mary Hooker. June at Smith college. New cycle, 8: 912. 1895. *5583.16.8

— Undergraduate life at Smith college. American university magazine, 3: 393. 1895–96. *7290.66.3

Jordan, Mary Augusta. Smith college. New England magazine and Bay state monthly, 5: 207. 1887. P R

— Smith college. Harper's bazar, 29: 678. 1896. . *5400.1.29

Lee, Gerald Stanley. [Amateur acting at Smith college.] Critic, 26: 355. 1896. P R

New woman's college, A [at Northampton, Mass.]. Scribner's monthly, 6: 748. 1873. P R

Suggests the adoption of the cottage system.

Seelye, Laurenus Clark. Smith college: its funds and aims. [Letter, reprinted from the Springfield republican, dated Northampton, Jan. 5, 1876.]

Smith, Sophia. Last will and testament of Miss Sophia Smith, late of Hatfield, Mass. Northampton, 1871. 4445.155

— Same. 1873. 4445.306

Smith college. N. p. 1877.
Reprinted from Scribner's monthly, 14: 9 [P R].

Smith college. Vassar miscellany, 11: 286. 1882.

Smith college for women. Unitarian review, 4: 191. 1895. P R

Tyler, Henry M. A Greek play and its presentation. Springfield. [1890?]

Ward, Alice. Home life at Smith college. The car window, 1: 162. 1883.
See also Hampshire county journal, published at Northampton, Mass., which gives annually, beginning in 1884, in its issue of commencement week, full accounts of all the exercises of the week, and of the growth of the college.

Syracuse. (1871.)

Alumni record. 1872–86. Syracuse, 1887.

Announcement of Syracuse university. Syracuse, 1871.

Annual, 1872/73–96/97. Syracuse, 1872–96.

Annual report to the Board of trustees. Syracuse, 1874–96.

By-laws. Syracuse, 1880.

Catalogue. 1896/97. [Syracuse. 1896.]

Special bulletin. [Syracuse.] 1896.

University herald. Vol. 1–25. Syracuse. [1873–] 97.

Haven, Erastus Otis. Statement of the Syracuse university. Syracuse, 1878.

Sims, Charles N. Statement of the Syracuse university. Syracuse, 1884.

University of Aberdeen. (1892.)

Aberdeen university calendar, 1892/93–96/97.

Bullock, John Malcolm. A history of the University of Aberdeen, 1495–1895. London, 1895. 2494.127

University of California. (1869.)

In 1868 the University of California was organized and approved by the Legislature; in 1869 the College of California, maintained as a private corporation, transferred its rights to the University.

Annual announcement of courses of instruction, 1886/87–96/97. Berkeley, 1886–96.

Annual report of the Secretary to the Board of regents. Sacramento, 1875–96.

Biennial report of the President in behalf of the Board of regents. 1868/69–96. Sacramento, 1869–96.

Register. 1870/71–95/96. Berkeley, 1871–96.
The university also publishes annual announcements and catalogues of the college of medicine, law, etc.

Berkeleyan. Berkeley, 1874–97.

Occident. Berkeley, 1881–97.

University of California magazine. Berkeley, 1895–97. 3 v.

Gilman, Daniel Coit. Statement of the progress and condition of the University of California. Berkeley, 1875. 2386.7

Heaton, T. L. How a university is building. Nation, 64: 85. 1897. P R

How to build up a university. Nation, 63: 494. 1896. P R

Jones, William Carey. Illustrated history of the University of California. San Francisco, 1895. *4490.109

Lovejoy, Arthur O. The University of California. Nation, 64: 47. 1897. P R

Plehn, Carl C. The growth of the University [of California]. Overland monthly, 29: 28. 1897. P R

Reinstein, J. B. Women graduates of the University of California. Nation, 57: 154. 1893. P R

University of Cambridge.

Examinations for women in 1872. [Cambridge, 1871.] 5592.79

Higher examinations of the University of Cambridge open to women. [Cambridge, 1887?]

Degrees for women at Cambridge. British medical journal, 1896 (1): 741. *7740.3.1896 (1)

Degrees for women at Cambridge, England. Nation, 64: 219. 1897. P R

Dickens, Charles, jr. A dictionary of the University of Cambridge, 1886–87. London, 1886. 2499.67

Fennell, Charles Augustus Maude. Cambridge degrees for women. Athenæum, 1896 (1): 845. P R
In answer to some remarks in the "Notes from Cambridge," on page 809 of the same volume.

Postgate, J. P. Shall women graduate at Cambridge? National review, 10: 191. 1887. P R

University of Cambridge local examinations, lectures, etc. (The student's guide to the University of Cambridge; 9: 52. 1882.)

Girton (1872) and Newnham (1873).

Entrance and scholarship examinations [at Girton.] 1887–97.

Girton college. Report, 1875/76–95/96.
Baldwin, Catherine. Women at an English university. Newnham college, Cambridge. Century, 42: 287. 1891.   P R
Blathwayt, Raymond. The education of our girls. Life at Girton college. Cassell's family magazine, 33: 410. 1894.   *7352.1.33
Bolton, Sarah Knowles. Higher education of women in Cambridge, Eng. Education, 2: 553. 1882.   P R
Cambridge M.A., A. Girton and Newnham colleges for women. Eclectic magazine, 97: 134. 1881.   P R
Davies, Emily. The proposed new college for women [at Hitchin, later Girton]. Victoria magazine, 12: 28. 1868.   P R
— Some account of a proposed new college for women [at Hitchin, later Girton]. Contemporary review, 9: 540. 1868.   P R
Davies, John Llewelyn. A new college for women. Girton. Macmillan's magazine, 18: 168. 1868.   P R
Field, Eleanor. Women at an English university. Newnham college, Cambridge. Century, 20: 287. 1891.   P R
Gadsden, Florence. Girton college. Vassar miscellany, 12: 198. 1883.
H. Women at Cambridge. Nation, 45: 51. 1887.   P R
Knatchbull-Hugessen, Eva. Newnham college from within. Nineteenth century, 21: 843. 1887.   P R
Ladies' colleges [at Cambridge and Oxford]. All the year round, n. s., 31: 111. 1883. P R
M., C. B. Examinations for women in Cambridge, England. Old and new, 4: 28. 1871.   .   P R
Magill, Helen. A girl student at Cambridge, England. Atlantic monthly, 42: 637. 1878.   P R
Meade, Elizabeth Thomasina. Girton college. Atalanta, 7: 325. 1894.   *5335.55.7
— Newnham college. Atalanta, 7: 525. 1894.   *5335.55.7
Minturn, Eliza Theodora. An interior view of Girton college, Cambridge. Printed for the London association of schoolmistresses. 1876.
Reprinted from the Nation, 22: 58. 1876 [P R].
N., N. Girton college and Smith college. Nation, 22: 112. 1876.   P R
A comparison: favorable to Smith.
Newnham and Cambridge. Nation, 46: 406. 1888.   P R
Newnham hall. Report, 1877, 85. [Cambridge, 1877–86.]
Newnham hall company, limited. [Report of the annual general meeting of the shareholders, June 27, 1877.]
This company, uniting with the Association for promoting the higher education of women in Cambridge, formed Newnham college.
Skelding, Eugenia. The first principal of Newnham college [Miss Clough]. Atlantic monthly, 72: 224. 1893.   P R
Wheeler, Emily F. The colleges for women at Cambridge. Good company, 4: 348. 1880.   *5375.5.4

University of Chicago. (1892.)

Annual register. July, 1893–July, 1896. Chicago, 1894–96.   *4480a.31

Quarterly calendar. June, 1892–Feb., 1896. Chicago, 1892–96.
University record, April 3, 1896–. Chicago, 1896–.
The University also publishes circulars of information and departmental programs.
Herrick, Robert. The University of Chicago. Scribner's magaine, 18: 399. 1895.   P R
Innovations at the University of Chicago. Nation, 55: 255. 1892.   P R
Judson, Harry Pratt. University of Chicago. Education, 16: 278. 1895–96.   P R
Laughlin, James Laurence. The University of Chicago. Nation, 55: 280. 1892.   P R
University of Chicago. Dial, 21: 31. 1896. P R
University of Chicago. Nation, 55: 216. 1892.   P R

University of Dublin.

Examinations for women. Regulations for 1896. [Dublin, 1895?]

University of Durham. (1895.)

Calendar, 1895/96, 96/97. Durham, 1895, 96.

University of Edinburgh. (1892.)

See also Section IV., Medicine.

Edinburgh university calendar. 1892/93–96/97. Edinburgh, 1892–96.
Grant, Sir Alexander, bart. The story of the University of Edinburgh. London, 1884. 2 v.   24903.53
Vol. 2, pp. 158–163, treat of the admission of women to the university.

University of Glasgow. (1892.)

Glasgow university calendar, 1892/93–96/97. Glasgow, 1892–96.   2509.116

Queen Margaret College. (1883.)

This was originally the Glasgow association for the higher education of women. The college was incorporated with the University of Glasgow in 1892.
Annual report. Glasgow, 1886–96.
Correspondence classes. [Circular of information. 1886?]
Memorandum and articles of association of Queen Margaret college. The companies' acts, 1862–80. Glasgow, 1883.

University of Kansas. (1864.)

Annual catalogue, 1866/67–96/97. Lawrence, 1866–96.   *4501.80
Sterling, Wilson. Quarter-centennial history of the University of Kansas, 1866–1891. Topeka, 1891.

University of London. (1878.)

Calendar, 1878–95/96. London, 1878–95.   *2509a.55
General register. London, 1889.   C.R.94.2
Regulations relating to the examinations for women. London, 1872.   5592.80

Barney, Elizabeth Cynthia. Women at the University of London. Nation, 58: 286. 1894. P R

Bolton, Sarah Knowles. Women in London university and in University college. Education, 4: 476. 1884. P R

Masson, David. University teaching for women. Victoria magazine, 13: 172. 1869. P R
This refers mainly to the University of London.

Morley, Henry. London university teaching considered from the modern side. (International conference on education, 1884, pp. 1–16.) *3763.100.15

Bedford College. (1849.)

Calendar. Session 1895–96. London, 1895.
Return [1893–4. London, 1894].

King's College. (1878.)

Calendar, 1895/96.
Department for ladies. Prospectus and syllabus of lectures, 1895/96.

Royal Holloway College. (1886.)

Armstrong, Walter. A woman's university. Art journal, n.s. 24: 24. 1885. *4072.205.n.s.24

University College. (1878.)

Calendar. Session 1895/96–96/97. London, 1895, 96.
College hall. [Residence for women students.] Annual report, 1–13. London, 1883–95.
Faculties of arts and laws and of science. Session 1895/96. London, 1895.
[Programme.] Session 1886/87. Faculties of arts and laws and of science. [London, 1886.]
Regulations for scholarships, exhibitions, prizes, etc. [London, 1896?]
Report [1893–4]. London, 1894.

University of Michigan. (1870.)

Calendar, 1870/71–96/97. Ann Arbor, 1870–96. *4486.2
Constitutional provisions, laws and by-laws of the University. Rev. ed. Adopted July 18, 1883. Ann Arbor, 1883. *4386.7
Exercises at the inauguration of President Angell and the laying of the corner stone of University hall, Ann Arbor, 1871.
General catalogue, 1837–1890. Ann Arbor, 1890.
President's annual report, 1870–96. Ann Arbor, 1870–96. *4501.55
Proceedings of the Board of regents. Ann Arbor, 1896.
Semicentennial celebration of the organization of the University of Michigan, June 26–30, 1887. Ann Arbor, 1888.
University record, April, 1891–Feb., 1895. [Ann Arbor, 1891–95.] *4490.108
The University also publishes regular announcements of the courses of instruction in the several departments.
The Inlander. Vol. 1, 1889/90–. Ann Arbor, 1890–.
The University of Michigan daily. Vol. 1, 1890/91–. Ann Arbor, 1891–.
Adams, Charles Kendall. Historical sketch of the University of Michigan. Prepared [for] the Commissioner of education. Ann Arbor, 1876. No. 1 in *4491.80

Benneson, Cora Agnes. Life of women at Michigan university. Woman's journal, 20: 244. 1889. *7260.51.20

Butterfield, Consul Willshire. University of Michigan. Magazine of western history, 5: 224. 1886. P R

Chase, Theodore Russell. The Michigan university book, 1844–80. Detroit, 1881. 2380a.55

Farrand, Elizabeth Martha. History of the University of Michigan. Ann Arbor, 1885. 2388.60

Garrigues, Adele M. The University of Michigan. Belford's magazine, Feb., 1890.

Hamlin, Sarah D. Michigan university. (Brackett, Anna C. The education of American girls, pp. 307–317 . 1874.) 3599.161

McLaughlin, Andrew Cunningham. History of higher education in Michigan. Washington, 1891. [U. S. Bureau of education. Circular of information, no. 4. 1891.] 3591.104
The larger portion of this work deals with the University of Michigan.

McMahan, Anna Benneson. Education at Michigan university. Woman's journal, 18: 366. 1887. *7260.51.18

— Michigan university. Christian register, 66: 740. 1887. *N.250.1.66

Salmon, Lucy Maynard. The University of Michigan. Vassar miscellany, Feb., 1892.

Scott, F. N. Entrance requirements at the University of Michigan. Educational review, 12: 184. 1896. P R

Sears, Edward Isidore. Michigan as our model university. National quarterly review, 32: 240; 33: 147. 1876. P R

Sheffield, Edith Lois. Student life at the University of Michigan. Cosmopolitan, 7: 107. 1889. P R

Stone, Lucinda H. Coeducation in the University of Michigan. Boston evening transcript, Aug. 14, 1885.
Reprinted in the Woman's journal, Sept. 12, 1885.

Ten Brook, Andrew. American state universities; in particular the rise and development of the University of Michigan. Cincinnati, 1875. 2386.5

Thomas, Calvin. The University of Michigan. The Western magazine, 4: 105. 1880.

Tyler, Moses Coit. Affairs at the University of Michigan. [The admission of women.] Nation, 11: 383. 1870. P R

— The University of Michigan. Scribner's monthly, 11: 523. 1876. P R

University of Oxford.

Most of the following pamphlets are to be found in the New York Public Library.
See also, under Section VIII, the Association for promoting the education of women in Oxford.

Admission of women to the B.A. degree. [Oxford, 1896.]

Admission of women to the B.A. degree. Resolutions to be submitted to congregation. [Oxford.] 1896.

Anson, William Reynell. A reply to the Camden professor [respecting the degree B.A. for women]. [Oxford, 1896.]

— Resolution (2). Diploma versus Degree [respecting the degree of B.A. for women]. [Oxford, 1896.]

Aristotle, pseud. To members of congregation [respecting degree B.A. for women]. [Oxford.] 1896.

Armstrong, Edward. Anecdota apologetica [respecting the degree of A.B. for women]. [Oxford, 1896.]

B.A. degree for women. [Oxford, 1896.]
— Same. Second notice.

Balliolensis. The due recognition of women by the University of Oxford. [Oxford, 1896.]

Bolton, Sarah Knowles. Higher education of women at Oxford university. Education. 4: 126. 1880. P R

Bright, James Franck. What is a diploma? (A few words about resolution 5) [respecting the degree of B.A. for women]. [Oxford.] 1896.

C., A. B. A personal explanation [respecting the degree of B.A. for women]. [Oxford, 1896.]

Case, Thomas. Against Oxford degrees for women. Fortnightly review, 64: 89. 1895. P R
— The real issue of resolution 4 [respecting the degree B.A. for women]. [Oxford.] 1896.
— An undelivered speech against resolution 4, Mr. Macan's papers of Feb. 11, and Feb. 27 [respecting the degree of B.A. for women]. [Oxford.] 1896.
[Circular] in opposition to resolutions for conferring upon women the degree of B.A. [Oxford.] 1896.

Conybeare, Frederick Cornwallis. University degrees for women. Academy, 49: 157. 1896. P R

Degrees for women [at Oxford]. Athenæum, 1896 (1): 118. P R

Dickens, Charles, jr. A dictionary of the University of Oxford, 1886-87. London, 1886.
2499a.106

Dodgson, Charles Lutwidge. Resident women students [respecting the degree of B.A. for women at Oxford university]. [Oxford, 1896.]

Dolman, Frederick. Women's colleges at Oxford. English illustrated magazine, 16: 459. 1897. P R

Due recognition of women by the University of Oxford. Papers against resolutions 1-4. Oxford, 1896.

Due recognition of women in the University. Reasons for voting for resolution 5 [respecting the degree of B.A. for women]. [Oxford, 1896.]

Fawcett, Millicent Garrett. Degrees for women at Oxford. Contemporary review, 69: 347. 1896. P R

Firth, Charles Harding. Resolution 2 [respecting the degree of B.A. for women]. A grievance and its remedies. [Oxford, 1896.]

Gent, Miss K. M. Women's education at Oxford. (Stedman, A. M. M., editor. Oxford, pp. 340-350. 1887.)

Gladstone, William Ewart. "Can the University stop, if it grants the B.A. degree to women?" Letter to the Vice-Chancellor of the University of Cambridge. [Oxford, 1896.]
Reprinted from the Times, March 13, 1880.

Grose, Thomas Hodge. Can the university stop, if it grants the B.A. degree to women? [Oxford, 1896.]

— Is it proposed to matriculate women? [Oxford, 1896.]
— Reply to Professor Case. [Oxford.] 1896.
— Some replies [respecting the degree B.A. for women]. [Oxford.] 1896.
— and Thomas Case. Oxford degrees for women. [Correspondence.] Fortnightly review, 64: 323. 1895. P.R.

Inferiority of the undergraduate course proposed by resolutions 2 and 4 to the freedom of education proposed by resolution 5 in the case of women. [Oxford, 1896.] .

Johnson, Arthur Henry. Some replies to Miss Maitland and Mr. Grose [respecting degree of B.A. for women]. [Oxford, 1896.]
— The "strict course" for women [respecting the degree of B.A.]. [Oxford, 1896.]

Macan, Reginald Walter. Diplomas and degrees for women. Oxford, 1896.
— A soft answer to the undelivered speech of Professor Case. [Oxford, 1896.]
— The value of a certificate for "the strict course," and the justice of the demand for it. Six reasons for supporting resolution 4. Oxford, 1896.

Maitland, Agnes C. The due recognition of women by the University of Oxford. [Oxford, 1896.]

Memorials and resolutions with respect to the admission of women to the B.A. degree, laid before the Hebdomadal Council in 1895 and 1896. Oxford, 1896.
In Oxford university gazette . . . Supplement to No. 854.

Oxford degrees for women. Spectator, 76: 334. 1896. P R

Oxford ladies' colleges. By a member of one of them. Woman's world, 1: 32. 1887.

Pelham, Henry Francis. An appeal [respecting the degree of B.A. for women]. [Oxford, 1896.]
— The new resolution (no. 5) [respecting degree of B.A. for women]. Reasons for voting against it. [Oxford, 1896.]
— A reply to the warden of All Souls, by the Camden professor [respecting degree of B.A. for women]. [Oxford.] 1896.

Report of the committee appointed by council on memorials respecting degree of B.A. for women. [Oxford, 1896.]
Reprinted from the Oxford university gazette, Feb. 4, 1896.

Resolution 5 [respecting the degree of B.A. for women]. [Oxford, 1896.]

Resolutions to be submitted to congregation, and reasons in favor of resolution 5 [respecting the degree B.A. for women]. [Oxford.] 1896.

Rogers, Annie M. A. H. A reply to Mr. Strachan-Davidson [respecting the degree B.A. for women]. [Oxford.] 1896.
— and Arthur Sidgwick. Women students at Oxford. Educational review, 3: 497. 1892. P R
From the London Educational review.

Sidgwick, Arthur. Letter which appeared in the "Times" of Feb. 11, in answer to Professor Gardner's letter of Jan. 31 [respecting degree of B.A. for women]. [Oxford.] 1896.

Sidgwick, Eleanor Mildred. Proposed degrees for women. 1896.

Statutes governing resolutions. Voting on resolutions [respecting the degree of B.A. for women]. Printed for the use of the members of congregation. [Oxford, 1896.]

Strachan-Davidson, James Leigh. University degrees for women. [Oxford.] 1896.
Student's handbook to the University and colleges of Oxford. 9th ed. Oxford, 1888. 2498.102
Pp. 258-264 are devoted to the education of women.
Suggestion, A [respecting degree of B.A. for women]. [Oxford, 1896.]
Thoughts suggested by "An undelivered speech" [respecting the degree B.A. for women]. [Oxford.] 1896.
Value of a genuine diploma [respecting the degree of B.A. for women]. [Oxford, 1896.]
Wakeman, Henry Offley. Some reasons for voting against resolutions 1-4, and for resolution 5 [respecting the degree B.A. for women]. [Oxford.] 1896.
Wells, J. The question of residence [respecting the degree of B.A. for women]. [Oxford, 1896.]
Women at Oxford. Spectator, 57 (1): 545. 1884. P R
Reprinted in the Critic, 4: 236.
Women at Oxford university. Andover review, 1: 658. 1884. *5325.5.1
Z. A noble resolution [respecting the degree of B.A. for women]. [Oxford, 1896.]

Lady Margaret Hall. (1879.)

Report, 1894/95, 95/96. Oxford, 1895, 96.

Somerville Hall. · (1879.)

Calendar, 1896-7. Oxford, 1896.
[Circular.] Oxford, 1881.
Report, 1879/80-95/96. Oxford, 1880-96.

University of the State of New York.

Annual report of the Regents [to date]. *6461.1
Examination papers for 1891/92-94. Albany, 1892-94. *3598.26
Proceedings of the 1st-25th convocation. Albany, 1865-87. *6361.2
1879 was never printed separately.
Regents' bulletin. No. 1-16. Albany, 1890-96. *6147.134
Hough, Franklin Benjamin. Historical and statistical record of the University of the state of New York, 1784-1884. With introductory sketch by David Murray. Albany, 1885. *6461.10
Sherwood, Sidney. University of the state of New York, origin, history and present organization. Albany, 1893. *4484.120

University of Wales. (1889.)

University College of Wales, Aberystwyth. (1872.)
Calendar, 1895/96.
List of resident women from 1887 to January, 1896.
Report. [1893/94.]
University College of North Wales, Bangor. (1884.)
Calendar, 1895/96. Bangor, 1895.
Report. [1893/94.] Bangor, 1894.

University College of South Wales and Monmouthshire, Cardiff. (1883.)
Calendar, 13th session, 1895/96. Manchester, 1895.
Report. [1893/94.] [Manchester?] 1894.

University of Wisconsin. (1868.)

Annual report of the Board of regents. Madison, 1868-82. *6403.35
Biennial report of the Board of regents, 1883/84-95/96. Madison, 1884-96.
By-laws of the Regents of the University. 1868, 70, 90. Madison, 1868-90.
Catalogue. 1868/9-95/96. Madison, 1868-96. 4494.27
General catalogue of officers and graduates, 1849-97. Madison, 1883-97. 4495.97
The Ægis. Vol. 1, Sept., 1886-. Madison, 1887-.
Daily cardinal. Vol. 1, Apr., 1892-. Madison, 1892-.
University press. Vol. 1-18. June, 1870-Oct., 1886. .Madison, 1870-86.
Allen, William Francis, and David E. Spencer. The University of Wisconsin. (Higher education in Wisconsin, pp. 11-44, 1889.) 4496.324
Butterfield, Consul Willshire. History of the University of Wisconsin. Madison, 1879. 2386.27
Carpenter, Stephen Haskins. An historical sketch of the University, 1849-76. [Also Catalogue of officers and graduates.] Madison, 1876. 4490a.8
Frankenburger, David Bower. The University of Wisconsin. New England magazine, 8: 10. 1893. P R
Frieze, Henry Simmons. The University of Wisconsin. Old and new, 4: 137. 1871. P R

Vassar. (1865.)

Addresses at the celebration of the completion of the twenty-fifth academic year. [N. Y.?] 1890. 4496.209
Annual catalogue of the officers and students, 1865/66-96/97. N. Y., 1866-96. 4496.14
Annual report of the Board of trustees to the Regents of the University of the state of New York. (Annual report of the Regents, 1867-96.) *6461.1
General catalogue of the officers and graduates. 1861-83. Poughkeepsie, 1883.
— Same. 1861-90. Poughkeepsie, 1890.
Historical sketch of Vassar college. Prepared [for] the Commissioner of the Bureau of education. N. Y., 1876. 4391.13
Items regarding its condition and progress, collated by the alumnæ trustees [F. M. Cushing, E. E. Poppleton, and Mrs. H. H. Backus]. 1889.
Laws and regulations. By order of the Board of trustees, adopted Oct., 1866. N. Y., 1866.
— Same. Adopted June, 1880. Poughkeepsie, 1880.
Proceedings of the trustees at their first meeting, in Poughkeepsie, Feb. 26, 1861. N. Y., 1861. 4496.322
Prospectus of Vassar female college, May, 1865. N. Y., 1865.
Report on organization [submitted to the trustees by the committee on faculty and studies, June 30, 1863]. 4492.126
The Vassar miscellany. Published by the Students' association of Vassar college. Poughkeepsie, N. Y., 1872-.

Vassarion, published by the senior class of Vassar college. Poughkeepsie, 1889–96.

Abbott, Frances M. A generation of college women [at Vassar]. Forum, 20: 377. 1895. P R

Associate alumnæ of Vassar college. Annual report, 1871–94/95. Poughkeepsie, 1871–95.

Avery, Alida C. Vassar college. (Brackett, Anna C. Education of American girls, pp. 346–361. 1874.)   3599.161

Backus, Helen Hiscock, and others. A few facts about the Vassar college of 1876. [By five of the instructors.] Poughkeepsie, 1876. Printed for private distribution.

Brackett, Anna Callender. Vassar college. Harper's New monthly magazine, 52: 346. 1876.   P R

Champney, Elizabeth Williams. Vassar college. Harper's bazar, 22: 155. 1889. *5400.1.22

Cincinnati association of Vassar alumnæ. To former students of Vassar college. [An appeal for the founding of scholarships.] By Truman J. Backus. From a former student of Vassar college. Before scholarships what? By Kate M. Lupton. Cincinnati, 1875.

Cohen, F., and E. E. Boyd. Vassar; a college souvenir. N. Y., 1896.

Freeman, Mary L. Vassar college. Education, 8: 73. 1887.   P R

Glazier, Susan Mariva. Address before the Philalethean society of Vassar college, June 21, 1871. Poughkeepsie, 1872.   4496.151

Hale, Sarah Josepha. Vassar college. Godey's lady's book, 73: 170. 1866.

— Vassar college opened. Godey's lady's book, 71: 173. 1865.

Hough, Franklin Benjamin, editor. Vassar college. (Historical and statistical record of the University of the state of New York, pp. 289–297. 1885.)   *6461.10

Jewett, Milo Parker. Vassar female college. The president's visit to Europe ["for the purpose of studying systems of female education"]. N. Y., 1863.   4496.202

Jones, Blanche A. Vassar college. New cycle, 8: 906. 1895.   *5583.16.8

— Vassar college. Frank Leslie's popular monthly, 43: 261. 1897.

Lossing, Benson John. Vassar college and its founder. N. Y., 1867.   4397.15

Lyman, Hannah Willard. Funeral services of the late Miss H. W. Lyman, lady principal of Vassar college. Montreal, 1871. Consisting of notices reprinted for private circulation.

— The Hannah W. Lyman memorial scholarship fund. Report of the committee [of her former pupils]. Montreal, 1871.

McFarland, Horatio Henry. What are they doing at Vassar? N. Y., 1871.   4492.127 Reprinted from Scribner's monthly, 2: 387. 1871.

Matthew Vassar, and the Vassar female college. American journal of education, 11: 53. 1862.   P R

North, Helen Marshall. A day at Vassar. Demorest's family magazine, 32: 404. 1896.

Orton, James. Four years in Vassar college. (Addresses and journal of proceedings of the National educational association, 1874, pp. 109–117.)   3596.50 (1874) Reprinted in the Victoria magazine, 24: 54.

— The liberal education of women, the demand and the method. Current thoughts in America and England. N. Y., 1873. 3598.54

— Vassar college. Old and new, 4: 257. 1871.   P R

Raymond, John Howard. Biographical sketch of Matthew Vassar, the founder of Vassar college. (Proceedings of the fifth anniversary of the University convocation of the state of New York, 1868, pp. 109–120.)   *6361.2 (1868)

— The demand of the age for a liberal education for women, and how it should be met. (Proceedings of the National Baptist educational convention, 1870, pp. 223–238.)

— Life and letters, ed. by his daughter [Harriet Raymond Lloyd]. N. Y., 1881. 4340a.127 Pages 498–744 relate to Vassar college during Dr. Raymond's presidency. Reviewed in the American, March, 12, 1881, under the heading, "The story of Vassar."

— Matthew Vassar. Galaxy, 8: 240. 1869. P R

— Vassar college. A sketch of its foundation, aims, and resources, and of the development of its scheme of instruction to the present time. Prepared at the request of the U. S. Commissioner of education. N. Y., 1873.   4497.240

Searing, Annie Eliza Pigeon. Vassar college. Harper's bazar, 29: 469. 1896. *5400.1.29

Sears, Edward Isidore. Vassar college and its degrees. National quarterly review, 19: 124, 381. 1869.   P R

Shall young men go to Vassar? If not, why not? Century, 33: 494; 34: 318. 1887. P R In answer to Professor Sill, Century, 32: 323. 1886.

Smith, Louise Russell. Social life at Vassar. Lippincott's monthly magazine, 39: 841. 1887.   P R

Tyler, Moses Coit. Vassar female college. Poughkeepsie, 1862. Reprinted from the New Englander, 21: 725 [P R].

Vassar, Matthew. Communications to the Board of trustees of Vassar college: by its founder. N. Y., 1886. Published by the New York association of Vassar alumnæ.

Vassar college. Nation, 10: 315. 1870. P R

Vassar college. Notes by a visitor. Old and new, 2: 115. 1870.   P R

Vassar female college. Massachusetts teacher, 14: 281. 1861.   *5286.1.14

Vassar female college. New Englander, 21: 725. 1862.   P R Considers especially the dormitory system.

Victoria University, Manchester. (1880.)

Statutes and regulations for degrees, examinations and courses of study. Manchester, 1881.   *6516.29

Owens College. (1871.)

Report. [1893/94.] Manchester, 1894.

Thompson, Joseph. The Owens college: its foundation and growth; and its connection with the Victoria university, Manchester. Manchester, 1886. Illus.   2490.75 Pp. 492–502 are devoted to an account of the incorporation of the Manchester and Salford college for women as a department of the Owens college.

University College, Liverpool. (1881.)

Calendar, 1895/96. Liverpool, 1895.
Report, 1893/94. Liverpool, 1894.

Yorkshire College, Leeds.

Calendar, 1879/80. [Leeds, 1879.]   2498.59
Report [for 1894. Leeds, 1894?].

Wellesley. (1875.)

Annual reports of the president and treasurer, 1895/96. Boston, 1897.
Calendar, 1876/77–96/97. Boston, 1877–96.
     *4393.63
Laying of the Stone hall corner-stone. Recent improvements in educational methods. The college and its work. Boston Herald, May 27, 1880 [morning edition].
Library festival. [Exercises of the day, with addresses by Rev. A. P. Peabody, E. N. Horsford and others.] Cambridge, 1886.
     *4492.182
Literary exercises of the alumnæ, commemorative of Henry F. Durant, founder of the college, at the Hotel Vendome, Boston. Boston, 1882.
President's report to the Board of trustees. 1882/83, 87/88–95/96. Boston, 1883–96.
Abbott, Edward. Wellesley college. Harper's new monthly magazine, 53: 321. 1876. P R
   Reprinted in Victoria magazine, 27: 542.
Abbott, Lyman. Wellesley college. Christian union, 25: 546. 1880.   P R
Barnard, Henry. Wellesley college. Notes of repeated visits. American journal of education, 30: 161. 1880.   P R
Bolton, Sarah Knowles. Alice E. Freeman. (Successful women, pp. 223–233. 1888.) 1554.16
Brimmer, Martin. An address upon the opening of the Farnsworth art school. Boston, 1889.   8073.39
Cook, Charles Henry. The effect of college life at Wellesley. [Read June 13, 1893.] Massachusetts medical society. Medical communications, 16: 191. 1895. *7737.10.16
Education of teachers at Wellesley. New England journal of education, 8: 8. 1878.
     *7590.8.8
Hill, Mary Brigham, and Helen Gertrude Eager, editors. Wellesley. The college beautiful. Boston, 1894.   4492.184
Horsford, Eben Norton, compiler. Souvenir of Wellesley college. [Opening of the Faculty parlor. Cambridge?] 1888. *4380.9
   Printed for private distribution.
Kinney, Mary Kendrick. Wellesley college. Harper's bazar, 21: 693. 1888. *5400.1.21
Lauderburn, M. D. E. Wellesley college. New cycle, 8: 885. 1895. *5583.16.8
McKenzie, Alexander. Wellesley college. Independent, 1885 (2): 1285. *N.713.1
Meredith, Mrs. Women's collegiate life in America: Wellesley college, Mass. Good words, 21: 838. 1880.   P R
Merrill, Estelle M. Hatch. (Jean Kincaid.) Wellesley college. Education, 7: 305. 1887. P R
New opportunities for lady-teachers at Wellesley. New England journal of education, 9: 432. 1879.   *7590.8.9
North, Helen Marshall. A glimpse of Wellesley. Demorest's family magazine, 32: 581. 1896.
Summer school at Wellesley college. Outlook, 53: 949. 1896.   P R
Thorpe, James Cole. The largest ladies' college in the world; or, a plea for the higher education of women. Churchman's shilling magazine, September and October, 1882.
Three years at Wellesley. New England journal of education, 8: 4. 1878. *7590.8.8
Views. Gardner, 1886. 24 pls. **K.180.18
Vincent, Louise Palmer. Outdoor life at Wellesley. Chautauquan, 11: 622. 1890. P R
Wellesley college. Its successful career and brilliant prospects. Boston daily advertiser, March 17, 1884.
Willis, Annie Isabel. A noted woman educator — Mrs. Alice Freeman Palmer. Education, 10: 469. 1890.   P R

Wesleyan. (1872.)

Alumni records, 1833–83. [Also] Supplement, 2d ed., Aug., 1895. Hartford, 1869–95. 4 v.
     *4485.57
Catalogue, 1872/73–96/97. Middletown, 1872–96.   *4496.17
Wesleyan university bulletin. No. 1–19. [Middletown, 1888–96.]   4496.264
Rice, William North. Wesleyan university. Scribner's monthly, 12: 648. 1876.   P R

VIII.   Societies for the Education and Advancement of Women.

Association for Promoting the Education of Women in Oxford.

Calendar, 1887/88–96/97. Oxford, 1887–96.
Constitution and rules. Oxford, 1895.
— Same. Revised to Feb., 1897.
Education of women in Oxford. A complete statement of the educational advantages now open. [Oxford.] N. d.
Home students. General report, 1879–95, and first annual report, 1895-6. [Oxford, 1896.]
Oxford university examinations for women. Regulations for 1896–7. [Oxford, 1896.]
Report, 1879–95/96. [Oxford, 1879–96.]
Women at Oxford. [Oxford, 1896.]

Association for Promoting the Higher Education of Women in New York.

Proceedings of the first public meeting. N. Y., 1882.

Association for the Advancement of Women.

Annual report, 5th–21st, 1878/79–92/93. Syracuse [etc.], 1879–93.   *7572.71
   The 21st report is entitled: Historical account of the Association.
Constitution and by-laws. Syracuse, 1876.
     No. 1 in 5574.29

— Same. Boston, 1877.   No. 2 in 5574.29
— Same. Worcester, 1882.   7586.27
Papers read at its 1st–19th congress. 1873–91.
  Syracuse [etc.], 1874–92.   *7572.70
  These papers have been separately entered under
  their respective authors.
Souvenir. 15th annual congress. Invited and
  entertained by Sorosis. N. Y., 1887. 5576.44
Gilliams, Leslie E. The Association for the
  advancement of women. Godey's magazine,
  132: 3. 1896.

Association of Collegiate Alumnæ.

Constitution. [Boston, 1882.]
Register. 1884/85–95/96.
  This contains the Constitution and the Annual re-
  ports.
Report of the 15th annual meeting, 1896.
  [Providence? 1897.]
Report of the committee on a basis of mem-
  bership. [Brooklyn? 1889.]
Report of the committee on admission of col-
  leges. N. p. 1890, 91.
Folsom, Ellen Minot. The Association of col-
  legiate alumnæ. (Papers read before the
  Association for the advancement of women,
  1887, pp. 28–33.)   *7572.70 (1887)
Talbot, Marion. The history, aims and meth-
  ods of the Association. [Chicago, 1893.]
  There are three Appendices. Appendix 3 contains
  a Chronological list of papers and addresses given
  before the Association.

Edinburgh Association for the University Education of Women.

Calendar. Edinburgh, 1886.

International Council of Women.

Report of Council assembled March 25 to
  April 1, 1888. Washington, 1888.
  Reprinted from the Woman's tribune, March 27–
  April 5, 1888.
  Contains various papers on the Higher education,
  Co-education, Woman in the professions, and Sex
  in brain, which are entered under their respective
  authors.

Massachusetts Society for the University Education of Women.

Annual report, 1st–19th. Boston, 1878–96. 7592.95

Society to Encourage Studies at Home.

Annual report, 1st–23d. 1873/74–95/96. [Bos-
  ton.] 1874–96.   *7590.12
Munger, Lillian M. Society to encourage
  studies at home. Education, 4: 547. 1884. P R
Society for the encouragement of home study.
  Vassar miscellany, 11: 402. 1882.
Society to encourage studies at home. Atlan-
  tic monthly, 38: 255. 1876.   P R

University Association of Women Teachers.

Elder, Constance. University association of
  women teachers. (Proceedings of the International congress of education. Chicago,
  1893, pp. 865–870.)   *3592.145

Woman's Education Association.

Annual report, 1st–25th. Boston, 1873–97.
          3592.126
  The 4th report was never printed. The 21st report
  contains a Review of twenty-one years' work.
Harvard examinations for women, 1875–79.
  [Boston, 1874–78.]   4483.118

Women's Anthropological Society.

Bulletin no. 6: Report of the section of psy-
Calendar for 1897. [Washington, 1896.]
Constitution. [Washington, 1896?]
  chology for 1894–95. Washington, 1895.
Organization and historical sketch of the ...
  society. Washington, 1889.
Proceedings of the one hundredth meeting,
  Jan. 28, 1893. Washington, 1893.

Women's University Association for Work in the Poorer Districts of London.

[Scheme. Objects of the Association, members, executive committee, and suggestions
  for work. London, 1887.]
Baldwin, Catherine. Some results of the
  higher education of women. Century, 52:
  958. 1896.   P R
  An account of the above association.

IX.   Periodical Publications.

American university magazine. Vol. 1–5 (no.
  3). Nov., 1894–March, 1897. N. Y., 1895–
  97.   *7290.66
  Successor to the University magazine [*7290.65].
Business woman's journal. N. Y., 1889–.
Englishwoman's review. No. 1–12; new series,
  vol. 1–. London, 1866–.
Englishwoman's year book and directory. Ed.
  by L. M. Hubbard. London, 1875–96.
  The original title was Year book of woman's work.
Frauenberuf. Monatsschrift für die Interessen
  der Frauenfrage. Weimar, 1887–93.
Frauenberuf. Zeitschrift für die Interessen
  der Frauen-Frage. Weimar, 1887–92.
  No more was published.

University magazine. Vol. 1–11 (no. 1–3).
  Jan., 1888–Sept., 1894. N.Y., 1888–94. *7290.65
Woman's journal. Vol. 1–27. Boston, 1870–
  96.   *7260.51
Woman's tribune. Vol. 1–13. Washington,
  D. C., 1883–96.
Year-book, The, of education for 1878, 1879.
  N. Y., 1878, 79. 2 v.   *3592.56
  The issue for 1878, on pp. 202–204, and for 1879, pp.
  122–125 have good summaries of the progress of the
  Higher education during these years.
Zeitschrift für weibliche Bildung in Schule und
  Haus. Zentralorgan für das deutsche Mäd-
  chenschulwesen. Leipzig, 1873–96.

AUTHOR INDEX.

www.ingramcontent.com/pod-product-compliance
Lightning Source LLC
Chambersburg PA
CBHW032123080426
42733CB00008B/1040